SKINWALKER RANCH
IN THE SHADOW OF THE RIDGE

BASED ON ACTUAL EVENTS

ERICK T. RHETTS

Also by Erick T. Rhetts

LOST ON SKINWALKER RANCH

THE MULEDEER CHRONICLES

SOPHIA

HUNGRY

IN THE NAME OF GOD

BETHANY GROOM—Into the Four Lands

BETHANY BROOM—Back to the Four Lands

Published by Prensa Tinta Azul

Copyright © 2015 by Erick T. Rhetts

All rights reserved under International and Pan American Copyright Conventions. Published by Tinta Azul Publishing. No part of this book may be reproduced or transmitted in any form whatsoever without prior written permission from the author.

Published in the United States of America

Cover by Erick T. Rhetts

In the Shadow of the Ridge	3
DR. WADE DIAS	7
GOLD COIN AND THE INTERESTING CASE	16
CARL AND DARRYL, PART 1	26
CARL AND DARRYL, PART 2	36
CARL AND DARRYL, PART 3	47
AUTUMN, 2013	59
THE DREAM HOUSE	69
IT'S NOT THE TELEVISION	80
THE SUMMER OF 2009	89
THE UNEXPLAINED DISABILITY	96
THE PORTAL	104
WHAT IT ALL MEANS	119

All characters or individuals portrayed in this work are attributed to the author. All semblance to any persons living or dead is purely coincidental.

PREFACE

Following the publication of <u>Lost on Skinwalker Ranch</u>—the option rights for which have since been purchased by a well-known and reasonably successful movie producer, I have had no few people with experiences related to the property, or the topic, reach out to me to share their stories. One of these stories led to me writing <u>The Muledeer Chronicles</u>, the narrative of which though not directly connected to the Skinwalker Ranch, nevertheless, tells the compelling and entertaining—though admittedly speculative—tale of one man's encounter with the paranormal, including a Skinwalker, the Holy People, and a rather threatening entity known to most as a shadow walker. Readers, however, seem to be more interested in stories directly related to the Ranch itself, probably due to the fact that it is a tangible location, than tales of the Skinwalker alone.

Unfortunately, since the publication of this second book, I found most of the stories and narratives being made available to me, while interesting, and yes, entertaining, were also to a large degree too brief to inspire a new book, and even then too repetitive for compilation. So to occupy my time, and to work through some of my own ideas, I wrote <u>Sophia, a Skinwalker Story</u>, an admittedly fictional manipulation of the real concepts but based (extremely) loosely on the events of one of those brief narratives. I'm afraid the jury is still out on that one; but if I may say so, it has its moments as pure horror, though subtle they may be.

In the interim, I was then contacted by Dr. Wade Dias, a professional psychologist licensed in the state of Utah. Dr. Dias started out our dialogue by telling me he had a pretty interesting story about the Skinwalker Ranch and asking if I would be interested in hearing it. Which, of course, I was. He prefaced by telling me that although he was willing to share with me some information which would help give the story credibility, there was a confidentiality issue. I simply assumed, at the time, that he was speaking of the doctor-patient relationship. And while that held to be accurate, he was more concerned with arrangements he had made with a nationally recognized organization with an interest in all things extraterrestrial and other-worldly. I had to agree in writing to honor this confidentiality before he would share his story. Which, of course, I did.

Then, as his story began to unfold, it became apparent to me that it was not entirely a "Ranch" story, and I grew hesitant. However, he assured me that if I allowed him to continue, I would see the connection. So I did, and I did.

For those not familiar, there is an extensive ridgeline which runs north to south through that particular part of Utah, and which the Native Americans residing thereabouts believe to be the path of the Skinwalker. The fact that Skinwalker Ranch sits within this stretch of rock is partially responsible for its name. However, according to many of the locals, the paranormal activity is not confined to the ranch alone. They believe that there are portals throughout the ridge which open to alternate dimensions or planes, and that it is through these portals that supernatural, paranormal, and, even perhaps, extraterrestrial entities move in and out of our world, and which account for the many strange encounters and unexplainable events which routinely occur in proximity to the ridge.

Dr. Dias' story is connected to the Skinwalker Ranch in this way. It relates the incredible encounters experienced by a family of five whose home was located about ten miles due north of the Ranch but nestled at the base of that same ridgeline which makes up the path of the Skinwalker. After hearing the whole of the story, I, too was convinced.

The intent of my preface, however, is not to tell Dr. Dias' story—that's the function of the book, but, instead, to ask of you, the reader, a certain willingness to suspend disbelief. The material provided to me by Dr. Dias was primarily in the form of clinical

In the Shadow of the Ridge

documents, informal notes, audio files, and transcripts. In order to then create the narrative style I wanted, I was required to use some literary license to "reproduce" certain elements of the dialogue between the individuals in the story. After all, other than the aforementioned audio files and transcripts, and these limited to Dr. Dias' sessions, it's not as if he or the other individuals in the story were otherwise doing the *Paranormal Activity* thing, filming and recording every moment of every day. I promise, regardless, the distraction is minimal.

I hope you enjoy the experience,
Erick T. Rhetts

DR. WADE DIAS

My name is Dr. Wade Dias. I am a licensed psychologist in the state of Utah. However, I do not engage in what most people would perceive as traditional practice. Not that I didn't ever do so.

Like everyone else coming out of college and going into the real world—that was in 1988, I started out by going down the same path traditional psychologist go down. For a good number of years I stayed the course, first accepting a position in the office of another, more established colleague, and then eventually opening up an office of my own. That office, as well as the one of my colleague, was in the city of Logan, in northern Utah.

In January of 2005, my wife and I headed south-east about 250 miles to Vernal. Jessica wanted to be close to her parents. They had a house at the end of a cul-de-sac south of 40. I acquiesced to her desire to be close, but not that close. So we bought a large house off of North 500 West. There's an awful lot of undeveloped land up that way; so you've got neighbors, but they're not right on top of you.

As soon as we moved in, I opened a private practice on East Main Street and not too far from the Regional Airport. I managed to secure a suite which took one-half of the second floor of a relatively new building. The other half was occupied by a chiropractor who was teamed up with a physical therapist. They gave me an immediate impression that their relationship went beyond professional, but I don't judge. Anyway, the first floor belonged to an architect and his staff. I didn't have much interaction with anyone there, just the occasional smile and wave hello. Everyone was very professional. It was a nice setup.

Jumping ahead, in 2007 I met quite by coincidence an older gentleman from Roosevelt. For those not familiar with the lay of the land in that part of the country, Roosevelt is just west of Vernal, no more than 30 miles, if that much. I was on my way to my office, having left the house a little later than my usual routine—no sense of immediacy that morning, and as I was tooling along 40, I noticed a motorist whose car was obviously not behaving up to expectation. The vehicle was pulled off to the shoulder, its hood up, and the up-to-that-point driver peering beneath with that look so many of us have when we really don't know what it is we're looking at.

Compelled by nothing more than my own good nature, I pulled off the road somewhat ahead of him, departed my vehicle and headed on foot in his direction. Now, I'm no mechanic either, so the best I could do after presenting myself in a cordial manner was offer him a ride.

"I can take you up to the service station," I remember suggesting.

His lips thinned, and he said, "I was already running late. I'd hoped to catch an 11:15 flight."

He looked like a nice enough gentleman to me. "If you want, I can give you a lift to the airport. It's on my way. My office is only a stone's throw from there."

He hesitated as I expected him to; who wants to bother a stranger? I headed him off before he could object. "It's no bother, really. Like I said, my office is right there. Two more minutes is not going to mess with my day."

"Let me get my things," he said, pushing the hood down tight.

I watched as he locked up the car, and with a small valise in hand, strolled back my way.

Like I said, he was an older gentleman, maybe late 60s. He was a tad taller than I, not quite six feet. He was definitely wiry, his shoulders narrow and with just a hint of the slopping that comes as we age. He wore Docker-like slacks, navy blue in color, his legs long, hips wider than his shoulders, and the rear pockets flat as a board. He wore flat-soled black shoes and a long-sleeved dress shirt, the top button undone. His hair was still primarily brown, but there were undeniable streaks of grey. There was, however, an agelessness to the depths of his brown eyes. It was that kind of thing where it's hard to pin down the person's age. I find this especially so of women, where their face tells you one thing, and their eyes another. That's why I don't try to guess their age.

"I really do appreciate this," he said, as he strode by me and towards the passenger door.

I guess he was in a hurry. I looked down at my watch and had to turn my wrist the other way due to the glare of the sun. It was 10:30.

We really didn't exchange anything more than some small talk on the way, but when I told him what I did for living, I could see by the expression on his face that he had come up with an idea.

"Say," he said, "if I were to leave you my keys, do you think you could get my car to the service station."

It was his turn this time to keep going before I could object.

"I realize it's a bit of an inconvenience, and you don't know me worth a hill of beans, but do this for me, and I'll make it worth your while."

I thought he was going to offer me some money, which by the way, I wouldn't have accepted. I do pretty well for myself, thank you. He was, after all, reaching for his wallet.

However, by the time I had moved my eyes back to the road and the pending turnoff for Vernal Regional, he had withdrawn what was no doubt the car's registration.

"My name is Brad Rogers, by the way," he said as he extended the registration my way and the car keys. No fobs those days. "I'm sure if you give these to the mechanic and tell him I'll retrieve them with my car when I return, there won't be any issues. I'll be back by Monday."

It was Friday morning.

What could I do, leave the guy hanging? "No trouble at all," I told him. And the truth was, it really wasn't.

I let him out in front of the terminal, and as he closed the door, he leaned in towards the open window and said, "I have a really interesting case for you. Not that I know your end of the business all that well, but believe me, this one is a doozy. And my people pay well."

He turned to leave, and then took a quick stride back. He then produced a business card as if out of thin air. At least I didn't see where it came from. "My cell number is on here, as well as my home and office. Perhaps you can give me a call and let me know where my car winds up?"

He thanked me again for my trouble, and that's where I left him.

For those interested in those kind of details, when I arrived at my office, I made a call and arranged for the local guy that I go to for oil changes and things like that to retrieve the car. We both had a good laugh about it, and he was kind enough to send over one of his mechanics to get the keys.

I said earlier, or at least implied, that I wasn't your run-of-the-mill psychologist. What I mean by that is that I tend to gravitate towards the more clinically singular cases, cases in which my subject's behaviors or challenges go beyond the norm, even for those, if you'll excuse the term, not normal. Most of these subjects are brought to my attention by lawyers looking for an unorthodox defense, doctors who have a tendency to do so with a smirk, or federal or state agencies wanting to know how to proceed, perhaps, with a grand jury.

I also implied that it wasn't always like this. Which is true. My first position had me working with the type of people you'd expect: stressed businessmen, unhappy spouses, people who couldn't sleep at night, teens who wouldn't respect their parents, substance abusers—I think you get the picture.

Every now and then, however, I would be handed or stumble across something out of the ordinary. Memorable among the first of these was the case of a teenaged girl by the name of Samantha Wilkins. It's not her actual name, but close enough. This particular case stands out, among other reasons, because she was the first upon whom I employed hypnosis. She was fifteen at the time, very pixie-like in appearance, and had been the victim of very disconcerting forms of abuse at the hand of her "stepfather" since the age of eight or nine; she couldn't quite remember. But that's all incidental to what made her so singular.

When she came to me, she was living with a foster family—two older folks—from south of Vernal, a neighborhood north of Fort Duchesne. She had been with them for about a year and according to the foster mother had been having nightmares.

Samantha, however, was convinced—and was rather convincing—that there was an entity of some sort that was visiting her regularly not in her dreams but in some dream-like state—and always at night after she had fallen asleep.

However, whenever I would bring-up this entity outside of the induced state, she would insist no knowledge of any visitations. Given her willingness to go into details about the abuse she endured—there she was rather graphic and at the same time so completely removed as to think she was narrating from the perspective of a disinterested observer, I had no reason to believe she was hiding anything from me. I could go into all the clinical possibilities as to why I might have been wrong, but it would be in terms of this story tangential.

I'd have to go back to my records to be one-hundred percent certain, but I believe it was the fourth or fifth time that I brought her under that she acknowledged the entity afterwards, meaning after having been brought out of hypnosis.

I simply asked her if she remembered telling me about someone in her room with her. Part of me was convinced this entity was a manifestation of her stepfather, an echo, as it were, of the subconscious repression of the abuse, or at the very least, the personification of her victimization.

"You dream, right?" she asked me rather rhetorically.

"Of course, we all do," I recall saying in a tone unintentionally textbook stiff. But she didn't seem to notice.

"Have you ever had a dream so real that you couldn't tell the difference?"

I shrugged with my eyebrows. "I think so."

"Not the long ones, but the short kind where you're dead certain for that moment that there really is someone there with you, that kind of real."

I knew exactly what she was saying. I routinely experience, even to this day, what I can only describe as a tangible entity which appears beside my bed or at the foot of it. So convinced I am at its actual presence, I awaken in the midst of kicking out, throwing punches, or attempting to push it away, with both my adrenalin and heart pumping. And while I realize at that very instant it's all just a dream, there's that momentary intrusion where I am convinced otherwise. The thing about it is that this presence has the appearance of being flesh and bone, yet somehow ethereal, with intense but fleeting physical detail and, well, presence. And while not necessarily malevolent, there is always the sense of a threat or an intention with which I am not at ease.

Of course, being a mental health physician, I rationalize these episodes as a manifestation of life's normal stress. So, "Yes," I said. But all the same, I was genuinely intrigued.

Regardless, it was enough for her to go on.

"Something—someone—comes into the room," she said. "It's not a person, at least not like a regular person, the kind you see in the mall, or sit next to in class, or even see on TV going about their business or whatever. But it is there and it is real."

I asked her if she could describe this presence.

She shook her head. "All I can say is that always for an instant I am sure I see his face, with all of its detail. But then all I am certain of is that there is something alien about him."

"You mean like ET?" I asked.

She shook her head and laughed, which I always liked; she had a nice laugh. "I don't think it's that kind of alien. More like—and this is going to sound silly—an insect or a critter from out of the dark depths of the ocean."

"But it looks like a man?"

"A man?" she repeated, as if testing the word for a fit. "Yes, like a man but not a man, and not a woman; I'm sure of that. By man, I mean, you know, with arms and legs, and a head, and all. Not that I ever see the arms or legs; maybe sometimes the hands. But I know they're there all the same."

Her description was uncanny in the sense that were I to be asked about my own nocturnal visitor, I'm sure I'd say something similar. Every time I experience this whatever it is, and only for the briefest of instants, there between awareness and awakening, I am certain of its features. But ask me to describe them or draw an image, and it's just not happening.

"Does this presence do anything? Does it say anything?" I asked.

She frowned indifferently. "He wants to use my animal."

"Use your animal? What does that mean?"

She shrugged her narrow shoulders. "I don't know. I don't even know how I know that that's what he wants to do, other than, like I said before, the way you know things in a dream."

I was about to ask her if there was anything else she wanted to tell me, but she had already started on.

Looking over my shoulder and out the window—it opens to the south, she said, her tone controlled and conversational, "There's this kind of dark glow behind him, almost like the halo of a candle burning. It's so dark that it looks purple against the black of the rest of the room. I'm not sure when I started to notice it, but I notice it all the time now.

"I think it's because he's there like every night that I've become pretty good at not getting all startled, crossing over the barrier of sleep, and waking up all scared, and he's not there anymore. It's like when it happens now, I know what it is, so I try not to wake, to keep the dream going. And that's how I got to noticing the glow, or whatever. And now when he goes, I get to watch. He just kind of drifts back away from the bed, and the dark closes around him, and when he does, that purple halo goes with him, too."

"When you say 'glow'," I asked her, "is there light, or maybe a reflection, for example like the moon, something that says this is light and this is dark?"

"Glow's just not the right word," she answered. "No, there is no light, not like that. I can't explain it." She sounded like she was getting frustrated. "I don't know the right word."

I down played it with whatever expression seemed right at the time. "We can talk some more the next time."

But we never got a next time.

Three or four days later, I received a visit from a detective from the local police department. It was a formal visit, but didn't last very long. She informed me that she had received a missing person's report on one Samantha Wilkins, age 15, and as she was a patient of mine, her foster mother thought maybe Samantha may have let on as to any plans to run away.

"Nothing like that," I said. "Are you sure she ran away."

She seemed indifferent, but answered all the same. "I can only go by the foster mother. According to her, the girl, as she did every other night, went off to bed. She says after that she neither heard nor saw anything out of the ordinary. But the next morning when she didn't hear the usual stirrings, she went and checked. The bed, or so it seemed, had been slept in. But the girl was gone. Nothing was missing. Even the clothes she wore the previous day were in the hamper. We've checked with the neighbors, and any friends we could find—not many of those. No one knows anything. Seems like she disappeared into thin air."

She asked a few more questions after that, nothing all that specific, and then left me her card in case I thought of anything later. But the truth of it is, other than on the odd or random occasion when something would bring her to mind, Samantha Wilkins was confined to an electronic file on one of the flash-drives stored in the lower drawer of my desk.

GOLD COIN AND THE INTERESTING CASE

My wife and I are childless, but not necessarily by choice. Which is to say if we had the choice, we would choose to have children. But fate is random, and whatever forces are involved bumped into us rather rudely and without pardon. After trying a number of times—intentionally, that is—and failing, we made an appointment with a very reputable doctor. Some tests later and he implied that having a child of our own, meaning together, might not be in the cards. He gave us some vague and general statement about an ovulation issue and said to give it time. The news upset Jessica deeply; she felt she was letting me down. Of course, that was not the case. The same randomness which turned up that particular card turned up the one that brought us together in the first place. We made a pact to remain optimistic; and of course, to keep trying, now evermore than before.

As for that first chance encounter, that was back in 1991. She was a history major at Utah State working nights in a small diner in Logan to make ends meet. I routinely ate at another place down on the other side of the highway, but office hours ran later than usual that night. When I came up to the usual spot, I noticed the flashing lights of an emergency vehicle in the parking lot and close to the entrance of the restaurant. If anything can kill an appetite it's the image of some overweight fat guy sprawled out on the floor and receiving CPR. I was resigned to going back to my apartment and having peanut butter and jelly. That's when I noticed as if for the first time the small diner a little further up the road, a place I passed every day but never gave a second thought to.

The place was nearly empty, which almost gave me pause for thought. But as I was already in the front door and the host approaching, I said what the heck. She led me to a booth more or less in the middle of the place and window-side overlooking Main Street. That's when I saw Jessica. She was wearing a pair of long slacks, black, and a light blue, long sleeved shirt with the diner logo and name across the top of the left breast—and what a breast it was. The rest of her wasn't bad either, a little too tall to be a gymnast perhaps, but definitely with a gymnast's body. Her facial features were small, with that little turned-up elfin-like nose that always gets my attention, dark brown eyes, and hair to match, styled short and straight. I knew immediately she was younger than I was, and probably by more than a few years—eight to be exact, but I also decided then and there it wasn't going to be a deterrent of any sort. I watched as she went over to retrieve a menu and then turned and came in my direction.

To make a long story short, we married four years later.

When I left the office, I made sure to drive past the service station. Sure enough Brand Rogers' car was parked out front and off to the side. Satisfied all was good, I headed home. By the time I got there, Jessica's car was up the drive and in front of the garage, which was separate from and in back of the house.

That she'd be home before me wasn't always the case. Back in Logan, she had taken a part-time teaching position at the University. Here in Vernal, she had initially planned on securing a teaching position in the public school system, but after a couple of interviews, the second of which resulted in an offer, she had a change of mind. Instead, she opened up a small curio shop dealing primarily in authentic Native American items, jewelry made from local and semi-local gems and stone, and other oddities that similarly odd people tend to be interested in. It didn't produce much in the way of income, but it was an enterprise to which she was deeply dedicated, and brought her into proximity to a subject with which she had always felt a deep connection.

She was there in the kitchen when I came in. As we both like to cook, we took turns preparing dinner, and that night it happened to be her turn. I gave her a peck on the cheek while she tended to the pots and pans.

"We're having steak and potatoes," she said.

I went in to discard my tie and then wash my hands. Back in the kitchen, I set the table—that was the other part of our routine, and then selected the appropriate beverage, which more often than not was beer. Jessica and I are connoisseurs, with a decided taste for Hacker-Pschorr, Spaten, and Mönchshof. If for some reason availability is in question, we'll settle for Beck's or Heineken, but preferably the dark. For this evening's meal, I selected the Spaten dark; it was a coin toss between that and the equally as wonderful Oktoberfest. For those who haven't had the pleasure, these are real beers, and a much more pleasant experience than any domestic swill can aspire to. When it comes to good beer, there's a simple test—if it is equally as satisfying room temperature as it is cold, then it's real beer. If the only way to choke it down is ice cold, it's Budweiser and not beer.

Jessica had prepared marinated steak bits with those small Russian potatoes, cut in half and sprinkled with salt and some dried oregano and then sautéed in butter and olive oil in a covered frying pan over medium heat—together a perfect match for the dark beer. As we sat and ate, she asked me if anything interesting had marked my day. I told her about Brad Rogers. She didn't find it all that interesting, but having mentioned it, I was reminded of the card he had given me, and that no doubt, he was by this time wondering as to the status of his vehicle.

"I'll have to call him after dinner," I said.

She looked up from her plate at me, her head tilted in that way. "I had an interesting day, too, thank you," she said with a pout.

She caught me taking a long taste from my mug. "Just thinking out loud, my dear. And so what was it that made your day so interesting?"

She smiled coyly as if she was deciding whether to fill me in or not. But we both knew better. "This old Ute came into the store."

"Oh, that is interesting," I said, being playfully sarcastic. "How rare for these parts."

"That's not the whole story, silly," she smirked.

I loved when she did that. "Oh good! I was hoping there'd be a little something more for my entertainment dollar."

"He came in early this morning," she said, "only moments after I opened the door. At first I thought he was homeless and had come begging. He was wearing this flannel shirt that was so faded I'm still not sure what color it was. It might have been red at one time, or even different shades of brown. I couldn't tell. His pants were nondescript, maybe even hand-made. I guess they sort of looked like jeans, but they were a faded black, not blue. And he was really dusty, head to toe, like he came in from out of the desert. And you had to see what he had on his feet. It looked like he was wearing animal skin moccasins with flat soles, only these came all the way up his shin like boots.

"I'm not afraid to say I was a bit unnerved. 'What can I do for you?' I asked, trying not to stare at him. His face was really weathered and sunbaked, with sharp creases under his cheeks and at the corner of his eyes. But it was the eyes that really got me; they were so sharp and feral, almost like the red-eye you get with photos when the lighting is not right."

"I'm sure that's what it was, the lighting in the store" I said, more so to let her know I was paying attention—which I was.

"Maybe, but I'm not sure. 'I have a coin,' he said, his words slow and his voice...I guess 'distant' is the way to describe it.

"I don't usually buy coins, I told him. But it was as if I hadn't said anything, or that what I said didn't matter.

"He drew the coin from the top pocket of his shirt and held it out to me flat in his palm. I didn't need to take it to see that it was real gold, and real old. I told him it looked really expensive, but that I'd have a look at it, if he liked. He kept his hand extended and waited for me to take it.

"I'll have to look it up, I said to him, gesturing to those books I have on the shelf there behind the counter—you know the ones. I told him again that I don't normally buy coins, so there'd be no guarantee that I'd have the proper resources to find its value. But he didn't say anything, just followed me with his eyes.

"The funny thing is, as soon as I had that coin in my hand, I knew I wanted to buy it. It had such a draw to it."

There was an excitement and even a hint of nervousness in her voice, neither an emotion to which she is easily disposed. "What kind of coin was it?" I asked her.

"A really old one, and from the looks of it south of the border," she said. "About the size of a silver-dollar, but heavier, thicker. And the gold was pale, not polished and shiny."

"What were the markings on it?"

"Designs. There weren't any words or dates. And it was roundish, but not contemporary round. My guess is Aztec, maybe Mayan or Incan. Definitely not Mexican—too old."

I took another long sip from my mug. "So what did you do?"

She grinned. "It's in the safe back in the store. I was sure the police were going to show up looking for it. And I still think it's a distinct possibility."

She has that kind of imagination. "What did you pay for it, if I may ask?"

She squinted a little. "That was odd too. He wasn't interested in money; he wanted to trade."

Not that I was going to say it out loud, but I didn't think there was anything in the store that had that kind of value. "So what did you trade?"

"He went right over to the display case down at the other end of the counter where the turquoise pieces are. It looked to me that he gave them the once over.

"Of course, I walked down with him. He then pointed out to me the ones he was interested in, waiting for me to take out the one before moving on to the next. He was very methodical. He picked out four pieces."

"Was there anything special about those four?"

She nodded. "He definitely had an eye for the real thing. You know that most of the pieces I stock come from the fairs down on the reservation. But not the ones he picked out. Those were the ones I bought from the museum when they were excessing inventory."

"Even then," I said, "it doesn't sound like an even trade."

She shrugged. "Wait. It gets stranger. He took only one. 'Let me weigh the coin first,' I said to him. I took it right over to the scale, but he didn't bother to follow. I told him it was 1.7 ounces, and that at the going rate, it was probably around $2500. And that's not counting the collectible value."

"What'd you pay for the turquoise?" I asked her.

"Maybe $300 for all four."

She sounded almost guilty.

"Do you think the old guy knew that, the difference in value, I mean?"

"I did my best to explain it to him. I even suggested he bring it to a coin dealer, or one of those places that buys gold. 'I have what I came for,' was all he said—no expression, no gestures, just those words. So I gave it to him and he left."

"Interesting," I said. "It sounds like he was on a mission. And then he just left?"

"He nodded by way of thanks. Funny though, I waited a second after he walked out of the shop and then went to the door to see where he was going, if there was a car waiting for him, or something like that. But the old guy must move faster than he looked, because when I got there, he was nowhere in sight. I even walked out onto the sidewalk. You know the sidewalk there. It's as straight as an arrow and there's really no place to go. But nothing. He simply disappeared."

I drained my mug. "Maybe he went into another store."

I could tell by the look on her face she didn't think so.

She looked at my cleaned plate and the emptied mug. "Your turn to do the dishes."

It was a little after eight at night when I made that call to Mr. Brad Rogers. His flight had taken him to southern California. I don't recall him saying exactly where, not that it matters, but that he was flying into Los Angeles.

He answered his cell on the first ring, so I guess he was expecting me.

"Hello, Dr. Dias," he said. "Hopefully I didn't cause you any more trouble."

"None at all, actually," I said. "The mechanic I take my own car to was more than happy to lend a hand. He's got the car now and told me he'd have it ready for you when you came for it. I have his number here, if you want to take it down."

Which he then did.

"Do you have a moment to talk?" he asked.

I was always in the mood to talk following a good mug of beer. "Absolutely."

"That case I mentioned. Are you interested?"

I had no way of telling, to be truthful, so I simply said, "Tell me about it."

"Let me preface," he said, "by telling you first that I am involved with an organization of which others tend to be skeptical, or at least of the subject that is the focus of said organization."

That was a hell of a start, but for me the right kind of bait. "Go on."

"I'm just going to come right out and say it. We monitor UFO and other paranormal activity." He then paused as if anticipating the silence which no doubt usually greeted him when making similar proclamations in the past.

Being a psychologist, I thought it best to let it play out that way, remaining silent for what I thought we be the appropriate length of time. "I'm still listening," I said, tinting my tone with a strategic degree of interest. Having met him in person, I was confident he was serious and not pulling my leg.

"What we need," he continued, "is the service of a professional and highly respected psychologist with experience in hypnosis."

"And you think I'm that guy?" I asked.

"I admit," he said, "when I met you this morning, and after our chat in the car, I was taking a stab in the dark. And please don't take this the wrong way, but since then I've had the opportunity to do some homework, and I now have no doubt that you're that guy."

I didn't take it the wrong way, but I was curious nonetheless. "I didn't know there was that kind of information about me available."

"It depends," he said, and somewhat cryptically, "who you know and the resources those people have access to. Let's just say I've learned enough to bring this case to you with confidence."

I paused for a moment, wondering who it was he might have spoken to. I then said, with perhaps the merest hint of annoyance, "I don't know if I should be flattered or paranoid."

He must have heard it, and quickly said, "The sooner is intended. So, still interested?"

I was, and said as much.

He sounded obviously pleased. "Good. Let me fill you in on some of the details, and then we can talk compensation."

Once off the phone with the good Mr. Rogers, I immediately found myself wondering if perhaps he was having a little bit of good-natured fun at my expense.

"A penny for your thoughts," said Jess as I nestled into the recliner to dumb down in front of the usual nighttime TV. She had made herself a cup of coffee, and there was one there on the table by my chair for me.

"That's all you're offering after your golden haul today?" I countered playfully.

"Tell me what you're thinking and maybe I'll increase the offer."

"The Rogers guy wants me to meet with a couple of guys who believe they've had an alien counter or something along those lines."

"Well, you are a psychologist," she said.

"Have you ever heard of UFO Ranch or Skinwalker Ranch? He tells me it's pretty close to here."

Jess thought for a moment. "I think so. There was a series of articles in the *Deseret* a number of years back. And I remember having an older woman come into the shop when I first opened asking if I carried corn pollen. She said it worked to ward off skin walkers. She also mentioned something about a haunted ranch and some upright dog-man running across rooftops down in Randlett or thereabouts."

"You're a fount of information. I don't remember you telling me any of that."

She smirked behind a sip of her coffee. "That doesn't mean I didn't, Mr. Attentive."

"You're right. Anyway, from what he tells me these two guys spent a night out that way. Apparently they had some sort of encounter, and the two of them are under the impression they were somehow affected, something lingering. He originally arranged for them to meet with a hypnotist affiliated with a UFO organization he is affiliated with, but there was some inside disagreement about objectivity, so they decided to go with someone neutral, as it were."

"Are you going to do it?"

I shrugged and took a sip of my coffee. It was sweet and black, just like I like it. "Of course," I answered. "I'm not one to pass up something this far out there, and he's willing to pay the going price and then some to keep it all confidential."

CARL AND DARRYL, PART 1

Carl was the taller of the two, and definitely more self-sure than Darryl. The day was a little more than two weeks after my serendipitous meeting with Mr. Rogers, the Wednesday following the Friday. They arrived together, although I had suggested separate means. The game plan was to interview them both together, and then do separate hypnosis sessions. The idea is that you want the process to be as objective as possible, particularly with regards to the results obtained under hypnosis.

They both, however, indicated there'd be no inconvenience, as they were staying together at a local hotel.

"This is our only mission here," offered Carl. "We drove down together, and we have intentions of being back in Logan sometime today."

That was a bit of unexpected information. "Brad didn't tell me you were from Logan. Both my wife and I are from there. Moved out here a couple of years ago. Her folks are here."

"I grew up there," said Carl.

Darryl nodded his head. "Me, too." He gestured with a lift of his chin towards Carl. "We met each other in high school and have been chasing weird shit since then." He caught himself immediately after, saying "Sorry for the language, Doc. I sometimes forget where I am."

I waved off his concern with a toss of my hand. "I'm not sensitive to it; don't give it a second thought. In fact, if it makes getting the point across easier, go for it."

His facial features softened. "Got it."

We made ourselves comfortable in my office. There's an area apart with roomy easy chairs, a nice center table, and large windows letting in plenty of natural light. I had already put out a tray of water bottles, some glasses—the tall plastic kind, and an ice bucket.

In the Shadow of the Ridge 27

I sat in the chair against the west wall and deepest into the room. Both Carl and Darryl chose the chairs with their backs to the window looking to the south.

To help you picture the two of them, Carl was a little taller than me, maybe 5'11". His frame was pretty much average, but he looked fit enough, and there was an athlete's flow to him. His hair was a light brown, but not sandy, layered over the back part of the ears, and tapered at the back to about the collar. It wasn't curly, but it wasn't straight either. His eyes were brown and serious. He had the full Vandyke, but it was kept close-cropped and the edges to the side sharp. He was casually dressed with light-colored khakis and a navy-blue button-less long sleeved shirt with no collar. I could, however, see that he had a tattoo on the topside of his right forearm, as it snaked, literally, downwards towards his wrist. He was to say later that he was 34 years-old.

Darryl was my height, 5'9, maybe a touch taller. He was of a smaller stature than Carl, and maybe 155 pounds. His hair was dark and thin. He wore it parted down the middle and long. As we sat there through our conversation, he was constantly pushing it back behind his ears, first one side and then the other. He too was 34 years of age, but his facial features made him look somewhat younger. His eyes were a glass-like blue. He was the more handsome of the two; not that it made any difference. He was dressed in a similar fashion as Carl, only with darker trousers and a lighter-colored shirt: no buttons, different collar.

I started off the formal part of our session by saying that Brad Rogers had given me only the merest details. "He was willing to tell me more," I assured them. "But I find it's best to go into the process with as little in the way of preconceived notions as possible." I then told them what Brad had told me.

They glanced at each other, and then simultaneously nodded. I took it as what Brad had told me was accurate.

"Before we get into greater detail," I said, "it would help me frame things if you'd both tell me a little about yourselves—nothing crazy, maybe a quick snapshot of your childhood, level of education, what you do for a living, and any other experiences perhaps related to this one." I then gestured to my cellphone which I had placed there in the middle of the table. "The usual disclaimer," I said. "We are recording; it's the most effective way to collect the data. I assume there are no objections."

They again exchanged glances, shook their heads in unison, and then as I had predicted to myself, Carl took the reins.

"I was born in 1973, like I said, in Logan. My father worked for the utility company and my mother was a supermarket cashier. The house I lived in was outside the city and away from the developments. There's a lot of wooded area out there, and some pretty cool hills and generally elevated land. When I was 13, I was out collecting firewood for the wood stove and our fireplaces. There were three of them in the house. It was towards the end of winter, mid-March, and there was some snow on the ground, but it hadn't snowed in a while from what I remember. Anyway, it was getting late, where the sky is that blue, dark-blue, but it's not yet night. I had left the ATV a little ways back, the other side of the deer run, and was cutting some smaller branches from a tree that had fallen."

I interrupted him. "You had an ATV?" It was more my own personal curiosity than any relevance to his story. Plus, I had always wanted one.

He smiled. "All my friends had them. Like I said, there was lots of woods and hills there, trails all over the place. We'd go riding all the time. My father had this trailer, too, that I'd hook up to the back to pile up the wood."

"So you were out there collecting wood," I re-prompted him.

"Right. And then I get this feeling something's watching me. There's all kinds of wildlife up there, so it's not like it's something unexpected. So I look around thinking maybe it's a raccoon or a deer, whatever. But instead, I see this tall dark figure up ahead, standing real tight to these trees. What's left of the sunlight, and it wasn't much, is to its back, so I can't make out anything in the way of features. It just looks tall and dark, like a shadow, only with three dimensions. This thing is like eight, maybe ten feet tall, but skinny, not much wider than the tree its standing next too. And like I said, I couldn't make out any detail, but I'd definitely say it was hairy, head to toe. Of course, right away, I'm thinking Bigfoot, because it wasn't a bear and it wasn't no man. Part of me is screaming run, and part of me is saying freeze. So I stood there with the handsaw down by my side and a rather impotent branch in my other hand. And just like that, the thing, the Bigfoot, turns and strides casually off into the darkness."

He paused then and there surveying my face for some expression he could evaluate.

"Did you ever see it again?" I asked, both my tone and expression remaining neutral.

He maintained eye contact and said, "I've seen others, but not that particular one, I don't think."

I nodded in that stereotypical and clinical manner which defines our profession. "Anything else you think would help me form the background?"

His lips drew straight and tight, like a man thinking. "I have a Master's degree, and these days I work in a field similar to yours. I am a mental health counselor, working mainly with people who have drug or alcohol dependencies, and also with those mandated by the courts. Other than that, there's my preoccupation with UFOs, the extraterrestrial, and just about anything paranormal."

I sat back in my chair and turned towards the other occupied chair. "Cool, and you Darryl?"

Darryl pushed up to the edge of his seat and leaned forward, his forearms on his thighs and his hands crossed. "I grew up not too far from where Carl did. But we were a little closer to those neighborhood developments he mentioned, though not in them. My family lived in the same house my father grew up in. He took it over after my grandfather passed away. So my grandmother lived with us too. All together there were eight of us: dad, mom, grandma, and the five of us kids. I'm the one in the middle, and none of us is more than 18 months separated from the one before or the one after. I guess you can say mom and dad got the kid thing over and done with up front.

"I was like five when we moved into that house. And from day one, even at that age, I had the feeling there was something else in there with us. Even now, I have no doubt that it is paranormal central; my mom and dad still live there, and grandma, too. She's 97, maybe 98. As for us kids, every one of us took the first chance we got to get out. We all go back there, for the holidays and things like that, but none of us stay too long. It's got that creepy feeling, if you know what I mean."

"Can you give some details?" I asked, gesturing towards the recording device.

He moved the hair back behind his left ear, then said, "Just the usual, I guess. Catching movement out of the corner of your eye, but then there's nothing there. The sound of low voices late at night when the house grows quiet, or even quiet laughter or sobbing. Objects routinely go missing, only to show up again in some part of the house they'd have no cause to be in. Other times things are moved around subtly, for example a flower pot from this side of the table to that side, or books are rearranged, though no one has touched them in years. Carl will tell you. He spent a couple of nights."

Carl nodded in acknowledgement, but he didn't say anything.

Interested in hearing more, I said to Darryl, "And this was all going on when you were little, and still to this day—when you go back, I mean?"

In the Shadow of the Ridge

He nodded, again pushing his hair back, but this time over the right ear. "I have to admit, though. It was a bit weirder when we were kids. More than once when I was sleeping, I'd be awakened by the feel of hands running over my body, down my chest, between my legs, my thighs, or even my back or butt if I was lying on my side or my stomach. I shared my room with my brother—the other three were my sisters, but we had separate beds and they were against opposite walls. And I swear, it felt like actual hands, skin to skin, if you know what I'm saying. All of us kids had similar experiences, but I'm the only one who is willing to talk about it."

I remarked that that particular recall was most interesting, and made a mental note to follow-up later if the opportunity presented itself. Until then, however, I wanted to keep the focus on the process at hand. "And your level of education, current work?"

"I did the junior college thing," he said almost apologetically. "I'm pretty good with computers and other electronics, so I do IT work for a friend's company. We service mainly small businesses and a couple of school districts."

Satisfied that I had enough background info, I said, "So that brings us to the events at the ranch. I've done a little bit of research, primarily the book by Kelleher and Knapp which Brad Rogers recommended. Other than that, my wife had heard some things. So if you can, provide whatever details you think might be useful. Then once we've concluded with this part, we'll go ahead with the hypnosis. You guys can choose who goes first, or we can flip a coin; it doesn't really matter—as long as we do each of you separately.

"Carl, why don't you start?"

He blew out a short puff of air. He then looked over at Darryl. "Okay, I guess it works best to start at the beginning."

"Yeah, just go with it," I said. "If you seem to bog down or are giving me details which seem off track, I'll just prompt you to move on. And neither one of you take that as anything personal; it's just part of the process."

32   In the Shadow of the Ridge

Carl gave me a casual thumbs-up. "Like Darryl said: we met in high school when we were juniors. We had a couple of classes together, one of which was English. That's where we discovered we had a mutual interest in the paranormal. We started to hang out together, and have been since then. Moving ahead, some years ago we made the official leap and got involved with a couple of different UFO and paranormal groups, some really formal and others not so formal."

As an aside he said, "These days, what with the internet, you can pretty much find anything you want to find."

I agreed and gestured he should continue.

"Right. Well, in 2005 Hunt for the Skinwalker came out. We had heard a little bit about a haunted ranch somewhere around Roosevelt or Fort Duchesne, and close to the rez, but really hadn't given it much thought. We were more interested in looking for Bigfoot in the elevations and woods up north. But after we read the book, we had to go have a look for ourselves. I mean they said it was the scariest place on Earth.

"Now this was just at the start of the fall in 2006, the last weekend in September. We both took off from work early that Friday—actually, there were three of us, Mandy too—and made plans to go camp out by the ranch, as close as we could get, for a night, maybe two."

I interrupted him and pointing at the recording device on the table, asked, "What did you know about the ranch at this time?"

He gave me the thumbs up again. "Really only what I read in the book, and some stuff from the newspaper. There were some articles in the *Deseret* by this guy Van Eyck. It was bought in the mid-90s by this guy Sherman. He moved in with his wife and two kids, and they were going to raise cattle. No sooner do they settle down, they encounter the bullet proof wolf who tries to eat one of their calves. Sherman, supposedly, fires at it a point blank range, and the thing simply trots off into the trees, the only sign it had

In the Shadow of the Ridge   33

been hit by bullets some matted hair they find on the ground. After that, three of his dogs go missing chasing after some entity or glowing object, and the family finds them the next day reduced to grease spots. After that, it's missing cattle, at least one of which seems to have been beamed up through some trees, the tops of which appear cauterized, or something. Then there's the UFO-type encounters, with flying and glowing objects of different size and shape passing over the property or up on the ridge. The wife even goes so far as to say she and her husband see a UFO of some type land on the property, or up on the ridge, wherever, and see some sort of extraterrestrial commandeering it. I believe there were a number of these type occurrences. Eventually, things get so bad, with disembodied voices and portals and whatnot opening all over the place, that Sherman sells the place to the hotel guy, Bigelow. With all the weird shit that happens after that, it just seemed a no-brainer to make the trip down that way."

"So the two of you go."

Carl shook his head. "Well, like I said, there were actually three of us. For credibility reasons, and for the sake of increased objectivity, three is better than two. So there was a third person, Mandy. We met her through one of the other groups, and she had been hanging with us for a while by then. She and Darryl were hooking up."

I looked over to Darryl, who confirmed as much with a lift of his hands.

"What was she like?" I asked.

"She's cool," said Carl. "Authentic and the outdoors type. From what she told us, she's Navajo on her mother's side. She had the look. And she's really into the UFO and paranormal stuff." He looked over at Darryl. "She's a little younger, though, right?"

Darryl nodded. "She's thirty, originally from Nevada, but she was living in Logan at the time—well, south of the city."

"If I can ask, is there any reason she's not here with us?"

Carl and Darryl exchanged glances. Then Darryl said, "She's back in Nevada. I reached out to her to see if she wanted to come with us—she's had residual issues too. But she said she was only interested in moving forward with her life and leaving everything else behind, meaning what happened out there."

It definitely added something to the mix. "So the three of you go out there. And it was the end of September."

Carl continued. "We had been told it was a bad idea to try and get on the property itself. There were guards, and the local police kept an eye too. We also were told to stay away from the ridge to the north, as it was private property, and that the property to the east bordered on reservation land, and the reservation police didn't take kindly to trespassers. So that left us the south and the west to find a place to set up, to camp. We were told there's a place called UFO Hill to the north and west, and not too far from Bottle Hollow reservoir, but that it was also pretty far away from the ranch. We wanted something closer.

"We had scoped the place out the best we could using Mapquest and Goggle maps, and thought for what we were looking for, seeing if we could sneak up close from the west would be best. There is a wooded area off the main road there where if we were lucky, we could get up right to the property line and not be seen.

"I don't want to say exactly where we were, but it was definitely to the west and in a copse of trees somewhat up the ridge and overlooking the north-west corner of the ranch property. It's possible we were on Hickens' property, but I'm not sure."

"Hickens?" I asked.

"He's the guy who owns the property to the north, where the ridge is that overlooks the ranch property."

I nodded.

"We got there right about dusk, around 7:00, I guess. The weather was good, low 60s, with a light breeze and very little cloud cover. We got off the main road on this semi-path which led into the trees. I say semi because it really wasn't much of a path. More or less just some passable terrain which led off the main road and into some trees, which were dense enough that once we got beyond them, there wasn't much chance of being seen from the road.

"We got lucky, as the path remained passable for a good hundred yards or so, and up a slight incline, yet still concealed by the trees. We made our way around a rock formation, but couldn't go much further with the SUV. So we parked it there, left our gear, and went off on foot a bit to find a spot which would give us a view of the ranch property, and if possible the ranch house, yet still keep us out of sight. According to the book, most of the activity happened in close proximity to the house, at least that's what we thought.

"We came up to some rocks and made our way to the other side, to the east. It brought us out into the open and we scurried for cover, as if there were guards patrolling every square inch of the place and we had been seen. Of course, we weren't. But that's the feeling we had going there. Crouching down together, we noticed not too far off what seemed to be the remains of an old house or barn. Other than weathered walls and a roof with little left to it, there was nothing else to say about it. We decided to set up our camp just the other side of those rocks, and out of a direct line of sight with anyone who might be down that way."

Pushing up to the edge of my seat, I suggested we pause there for a moment indicating the tray with the bottles. I for one was in need. "The water is cold," I invited. "And there's ice, too."

They both took me up on the offer, grabbing a bottle but passing on the glass. "You don't mind," said Carl, twisting off the cap.

"Not a bit. They're there in case you want ice."

CARL AND DARRYL, PART 2

We spent a moment in small talk while I checked the recording device and made sure everything was copasetic, which it was. The volume was good and our voices clear. I then did a quick review aloud of what we had covered, and then asked who was going to continue.

It was Carl. "Okay, so right after that, we went back and started setting up camp. We choose a spot about a hundred feet or so from the SUV and close to the rocks. There was some sparse grasses and stuff carpeting the ground so that the tent floor wouldn't be on hard stone or packed dirt. There were also a couple of thin trees, so it had the look of the right place to put up a tent. Besides, Darryl and I had done this a bunch of times before on other paranormal adventures.

"The tent we had was one of the bigger ones, eight by eight at the base, and I guess a little less in height, at least directly overhead. We got the support poles in place and spiked the corners and sides into the ground. Like I said, the weather was pretty mellow, so there weren't any real concerns it was going to blow over, or anything like that.

"Once the tent was up, and that took about an hour, that and putting all our other shit in order, we scoured about for firewood, of which there was plenty. We got the fire going, keeping it small and close to the rocks; but we weren't really worried about being seen. The ranch house was all the way on the other side of the property, which was probably a mile away, give or take.

"After that, we just settled in. We made something to eat, and sat out in some chairs to watch the skies. We had no doubt we were in for some spectacular shit, giving all we had heard. I'm not afraid to say it: we were definitely expecting little green men or something equally as mind-blowing."

In the Shadow of the Ridge 37

He paused and took a drink from the bottle, wetting his lips with his tongue.

"This is where things start getting a little out of the ordinary," he said to continue. "The three of us are sitting there each with a different perspective of the sky. There's no sense in us all looking in the same spot. By this time, it is fully night, but the sky is not as dark as you'd think, and not because of the moon or because it's full of stars. It was just an odd type of light.

"But there's nothing going on, nothing to see, anyway. But then Darryl, out of the blue, makes this comment that he feels funny. Funnier still, is it turns out we're all feeling that way. The way I can best describe it—and Darryl feel free to chime in here, it was as if I was stoned."

He looked over at me as if unsure.

"I don't know if you've ever been, Doc."

He waited.

"I went to college too," I said.

It was enough. He went on. "Well then, you know what I'm getting at. It was as if my senses had been muted, as if I had become detached from myself, even if only a little. The other two, Darryl and Mandy, said they felt the same."

Carl glanced over at Darryl, who was pushing his hair back behind his right ear.

Darryl nodded. "It was definitely a sensory perception thing. Our cognitive functions seemed to have been suppressed, while our emotional responses were heightened. It was, in a way, kind of feral, if you know what I'm saying." Then he quickly added, "And we weren't stoned or drunk. We take this UFO shit seriously, like a real science, so we don't bring anything with us that can influence what we see or experience."

He then gestured for Carl to resume what he was saying.

"It was right about the same time that we saw this orange glow kind of edge the sky. But it wasn't this full-blown light. It was only there at the edges of our vision, peripherally, I guess, is the word. It was east of our position and to the other side of the rocks. None of us, however, were inclined to get up out of our chairs and go have a look. Instead, we sat there acting silly, like school kids, and at the same time experiencing a bit of fear, but not of anything specific."

"I'm not sure if fear is the right word," said Darryl, but not in any way judgmental. "But there was definitely some tangible anxiety."

Carl turned up his palm in that way the signals neither agreement nor disagreement.

"But whatever it was," Carl went on. "It didn't last long, only that feeling we all shared that something was weighing down upon us or creeping into us in some way.

"We sat out there for a few more hours, certain that something awesome was going to happen at any time. But outside of sporadic ghost lights, we didn't see anything that met our expectations going in."

Ghost lights was an expression I had never heard before, so I asked.

"They're light orbs which can vary in size, but the type we see out here are baseball sized, maybe basketball sized. More often than not they are bluish in color, but could be yellow or even red. They seem to hover and dart about just over the surface of the ground, or up in the trees. I've done some research on the subject. There are others that call them earth lights or more scientifically, anomalous luminous phenomena. One of the theories is they are the product of tectonic strain along faults in the bedrock. UFO and paranormal seekers prefer to think of them as something else, the presence of unexplained entities, for example."

Again Darryl found something to add. "But there was this flash, sort of a light echo, which did light up the underside of the clouds above the ranch property. It was pretty weird, because whatever the source, it came from the ground up, and not the other way around."

"And that's what I'm talking about," said Carl. "There we were, out there looking for weird shit, and weird shit happens, and it was like, 'so what?' None of us had any desire to get up and go look, as if we were being controlled. Something had anesthetized us, in a way, an emotional anesthetic. It's like Novocain at the dentist. You know the pain is there, but you're just not feeling it.

"Then right before we were ready to call it a night and get some sleep, somewhere around 3:00 in the morning, maybe a little after, we saw this much larger orb. It wasn't any ghost light. This was at least the size of a car."

"Bigger," interjected Darryl. "A good sized truck is more like it—and not a pickup, but like a delivery truck."

Carl conceded with a short flick of his fingers. "You definitely got a longer look at it than me." Turning to me, he added, "From where I was seated, the rocks were in the way. He and Mandy were more out in the open and had a better line of sight."

Darryl shook his head in acknowledgement. "It sort of appeared out of nowhere, and then just as suddenly moved off towards the ranch house, but not as if it was in any hurry. I watched it for a good two or three seconds before it went out of sight. There are a couple of tree lines that run through the middle of the fields there on the property, but I can't say, at least at the time, if that's what happened, it sank below the tree line. All I know, is that I was just then overcome by a pretty intense feeling of depression."

I turned to look over at Carl, whose eyes were intently fixed on Darryl. I caught his attention.

"Did you feel it too, Carl, the depression?"

He didn't immediately look my way, but answered, "More than anything, I recall feeling out of it, as if drugged, like a heavy tarp had been dropped over my senses."

He then paused as if waiting on Darryl, kind of the way two people act when they've told the same story together a number of times, and it's the other guy's line. When a short time passed without a word from either of them, I said, "Is that all?"

"Darryl, tell Doc about what you saw, you and Mandy."

"This is a little fucked up," he said. "We still haven't figured out why Carl didn't see it, when we did. It was clear as day, even in the dark. What it was was a bird. At least it looked and moved like one. But it was huge, much bigger than anything I've ever seen around here. Mandy and I saw it at the same time. There was a bluish glow to it, but really dim, and shimmering, almost as if it was radiating a reflection from some other source. It sort of rose up over the area where the old homestead is that we told you about. And then it went up and over the top of the ridge and was gone. A couple of seconds, and that was it."

"How big was it?" I asked.

"I'd say the wing span was a good ten feet, but I'm only going by what I saw glowing."

"And Mandy saw it too, but not Carl?"

"She saw it. I mean, we immediately looked at each other, and we both had these silly grins on our faces."

"I must have been out of it, or something," said Carl. "I don't recall them seeing it at the time, but that was only a matter of seconds, too. I just sort of brushed it off to zoning out. Like I said, it was getting late, and we were set to call it a night."

"Did anything further of note take place before you actually did?"

Carl shook his head. "No, that was it. We put the fire out, covering it with a good inch or two of dirt to make sure. First, we didn't want anyone patrolling the ranch to see the smoke, and two, we didn't want any wayward embers to set the surrounding trees on fire.

"Inside the tent, we had laid our sleeping bags the long way so that we were all facing the opening. Darryl and Mandy were side by

In the Shadow of the Ridge   41

side to one side, and I was on the other so that there was some space to move around between us.

"We didn't go straight off to sleep, leaving the light on to allow us to get into the sleeping bags, and then just spent some time talking. I even took the time to make sure that the tent flap was zipped all the way and the snaps were done up at the bottom. I had no desire to be awakened by some curious creature smelling my breath.

"We were just hanging out, talking about our plans for the next day—we were debating whether to stay another night or head home, when we all heard what sounded like a guy clearing his throat or maybe coughing. It sounded really close. So we all got real quiet, and sat there listening to the night. And we heard it a second time, the same sound. Darryl remarked that it could be one of the guards we were told about nearby, but not that nearby. 'Voices carry out here,' he said. 'He could be a few hundred yards away, and we'd still hear it as if he was on top of us.' Shortly after that, the very top of the tent caught some light, as if a beam was shining over the top of the rocks, and we heard the unmistakable sound of a car motor. We assumed it was one of their vehicles coming up that dirt road. I can't really say. Regardless, it was gone as quickly as it came.

"Later on we heard some coyotes sniffing around outside, and from what it sounded like, fairly close to the tent. But they too went off without any encouragement from us. It was a bit unnerving to have them so close, but we were in the desert, after all; so there was nothing all that strange about it.

"And that's when the campfire flared up, all by itself. And not a little flame, but a big one—big enough that it lit up the front flap of the tent from fifteen feet away. So I turned to Darryl and said that I definitely saw him extinguish it, saw it with my own eyes. Under two inches of dirt, he reminded me."

I glanced over at Darryl who was pushing his hair back, but also nodding in agreement.

Carl continued, "While we sat there debating who was going to go and put it out, all three of us clearly heard something moving around out there. And it was no coyote. Whatever it was was walking heavy and making no effort to conceal its presence. I saw Darryl was about to say something, and put my finger against my lips, and was shaking my head 'no'. I didn't know what was out there, but I knew I didn't want it in the tent with us.

"It plodded around to the other side of the tent—we could all hear it clear as day; and then I guess it just walked off. We weren't hearing any more footsteps or stirring. That's when we noticed the fire had gone out again.

"Anyway, that's the way we left it. It was as if it didn't really matter; we were indifferent to whatever was going on, and not because we wanted to be, but looking back on it, it was as if none of it was under our control.

"I don't remember actually falling asleep, but I do remember lying there for a bit listening to the soft breathing of both Mandy and Darryl, and I remember remarking to myself that they must have really been tired given how fast they both nodded out.

"What I do remember is waking up rather suddenly and having an urgent need to piss, as if I had drank a six pack of beer. Just as I was getting out of my sleeping bag, Darryl turned over towards me, his eyes still shut by sleep, and said in this really harsh whisper, 'No fucking way. No fucking way.' He then sat straight up, had this really fucked up look on his face, like he was scared shitless. His eyes shot wide open, and then closed just as quickly. And like that, he laid back down as peacefully as you could imagine, as if nothing had happened.

"I thought about shaking him awake, but my bladder felt like it was going to burst. So I got the tent flap undone and headed out to the trees the other side of the SUV. By the time I got out there, I had to piss so bad I almost couldn't get it started. Finally, it just came, crackling steadily down into the dirt at the base of the tree I picked. So intent was I on the relief that came with it that at first I was oblivious to anything else. But then, just like that, I was fully aware of someone standing to my back. Obviously, my first thought was it was Darryl or even Mandy. It's not like I had a monopoly on pissing on a tree.

"With my stream still going steady, I turned my head the best I could to look over my shoulder and still be aiming at something other than my bare feet. What I saw cut me off like that." He snapped his fingers. "There behind me was this amorphous shape, black against the blackness. It had to be no less than seven feet tall and easily as wide as two big men. I let myself go and did a panic turn to face it up. It just stood there about fifteen feet from me, there where the ground was open and flat. That's when I realized I couldn't move. I'm not even sure how I was managing to stay on my feet. And I swear, I never saw the thing move, and the next thing I know, it's kind of half-squatting, half bending over towards me, and less than a half-foot away from my face. All I remember after that is trying to catch my breath, as if I was breathing in mud, or if I had a thick plastic bag pulled over my head.

"The next thing I know, there's sunlight seeping in through the open flap of the tent while I'm lying there on top of my sleeping bag, the better part of me in a somewhat excited state and poking more than a little through the opening of my boxers, and my pants still unbuttoned and the zipper all the way down. That's when I remembered being by the bushes and whatever it was that was out there with me.

"Strangely enough, because I don't remember drinking any water after the first time, I again had to piss. This time I went out just to the other side of the tent. The sun was already above the ridge to the east. I looked around to see if there was anything out of place, but it was all cool. I took my piss and went back into the tent, all the while noticing that my throat was awfully sore, as if I had spent the night breathing in smoke. You know, like that irritating feeling you get if you're in proximity to burning leaves for too long, or when smoke lingers from a forest fire. Something like that.

"When I got back into the tent, both Darryl and Mandy were out of their sleeping bags and throwing some clothing on. I asked how they felt, wondering if I was the only one not feeling up to par. They too mentioned sore throats and a sort of pressure between the eyes. I too felt that, but I thought it was just the morning air.

"We put up a pot of coffee, and as we sat there sipping from those tin camping cups, one thing led to another, and I told them about what I thought had happened to me. That's when Darryl shared that he had some kind of weird dream, although it seemed a little too real."

Carl stopped here and suggested Darryl take it from there.

Darryl sat up to the edge of the chair again, and this time pushed back both sides of his hair at the same time. "There's not much to say, really. I thought I saw something come into the tent. It was crawling or slithering towards Mandy. But it wasn't a snake or anything small like that. It was big, as big as any normal person. I watched as it slithered or crawled up alongside of her. All I know is I wanted to reach out and pull her towards me, or, I don't know, push the thing away. But I had no control over any of my body parts. I could feel myself trying to lift my arms, but they felt so heavy, so far away from me, that all I could do was lie there and watch. This thing—and I can't recall a single detail other than what I've already told you, did something with her mouth. But she was facing away from me, so I couldn't tell what it was. All I remember after that was thinking what a really odd dream that was. I think I sat up after that. But even now I'm not sure. As far as I know, I went back to sleep, and really didn't think about it until Carl told us about his thing while taking a piss."

In the Shadow of the Ridge

"Did you stay another night?"

Carl shook his head. He then drained what was left in the bottle he held, and continued. "No. We were all feeling this dread or anxiety, like there was some presence all around us. I'm not saying we felt threatened, but definitely vulnerable, like whatever was out there was taking some time to decide. So we decided to act first. We finished our coffee, and then immediately got to breaking down the campsite. And that's when Darryl noticed that the ground beneath the tent where our sleeping bags had each lain was changed. The grass and shit that was growing there was completely shriveled and colorless like fungus, the kind that grows where there's no light. He used his cellphone to take some photos, and then we threw all of our stuff into the SUV and got out of there.

"We had no intention of driving back to Logan all in one trip, so we were heading towards a breakfast place that we had seen on the way down. It was only about 15-20 miles up the highway there. And that's when the weirdness got even weirder. All three of us felt the need to urinate, and we pulled over at least twice more on the way. And not only that, but we also had simultaneous nose bleeds; and I for one, never get nosebleeds."

"I've had them before," chimed in Darryl. "But usually only as a result of a cold, or if the air is really dry for an extended spell. But even then, they don't last. I squeeze my nostrils for a few seconds, and it stops. But not this one. No matter how much squeezing I did, it continued to trickle."

"Same with me, and the same with Mandy," said Carl. "But by the time we got to the food stop, the bleeding had stopped. We all felt a bit light-headed, with that same pressure between the eyes. We went inside and ordered breakfast, but none of us had much of an appetite. We were sure something bizarre had happened to us, and that whatever it was, it was significant."

It was a lot to take in, I have to admit. "And so that's why you are here?"

"Basically, yeah. We both feel something happened to us out there." He tapped at his temple with the tip of his index finger. "It's locked up in here someplace, and needs to be drawn out. For the last couple of months, all three of us have been experiencing the same shit: depressed cognitive function, hyper-sensitive emotional response, a vague feeling of anxiety; and every time we try to talk about it, even just the three of us, or these days Darryl and I, we get this tremendous pressure build-up right here between the eyes." He took to tapping his forehead. "And as soon as we let the topic drop, the pressure stops."

"How about now?" I asked. "Do you feel anything? You are talking about it."

He shook his head.

"How about you, Darryl?"

"No, it's all good."

CARL AND DARRYL, PART 3

I called Brad Rogers that evening from my home, referring to the pages of my notes that I had printed up prior to leaving my office. I also made scans of the drawings both Carl and Darryl produced under hypnosis, saved them to file, and emailed them to myself here at the house.

"You had them make drawings?" Rogers asked when I told him I was in the process of sending them to him.

"It's routine in situations like this," I assured him.

"And what if the patient can't draw?" He asked with a chuckle.

"Believe it or not," I told him, "what hampers people from exhibiting spatial intelligence such as producing accurate depictions is all psychological. They over think it and become more preoccupied with the three dimensional challenge, instead of just drawing what they see. Under hypnosis, that sort of obstacle is pretty much removed. Now, I'm not saying you get Picasso or Dali, but I think you'll be impressed. You should be getting them any second now, if they haven't come through already. I assume you'll be able to open them up on your cell, but if not, definitely your laptop or PC—assuming you have one."

"I have my laptop right here; I'll let you know when they come through. Until then, what's your take on all of this?"

For the next twenty minutes or so, I told him about the interview process, sharing with Rogers some of the details. It was obvious that he had heard their story before, as he was confirming or comparing what it was I was telling him with what he already knew.

"That's one of the things I'm most impressed by. They pretty much tell it the same way every time, but with enough variation in the little things to suggest none of it is rehearsed."

I agreed that I didn't think they were trying to put one over on anyone.

"Now tell me about the other part, the details that came out under hypnosis."

He was clearly as eager to hear about it as I was to tell him.

"Well, Carl went first," I said. "And he was highly susceptible to the process. I use a fairly traditional induction method and his eyes went wavy literally in a matter of seconds, his eyelids fluttered a few times, and he was under.

"I led him along using the details which he provided in the interview, guiding him to focus on those objects he would have confined to his peripheral vision during the event, and using specific words and expressions he himself used during the interview as suggestion. The idea is to narrow the vision of his memory to fields he may have paid little mind to at the time, either somewhat consciously because he was intent on some other stimuli, or subconsciously because he may not have been in full control of his own cognitive faculties."

I paused a moment to give Rogers a chance to express himself if he had the need.

"I follow what you're saying," he said. "It sounds similar to other hypnotherapists with whom I have worked."

"Good. The first detail that surfaced, which did not surface during the interview, was the sudden appearance of an insect-like entity which apparently accosted Darryl. This event occurred while the three of them were seated outside the tent and in vicinity of the campfire. From what Carl said, this thing slid about the air over their heads before it seemingly and suddenly targeted Darryl. It went straight towards him, seemed to deflect off the surface of the ground, and then attached itself to the back side of Darryl's pant leg, at the calf, and biting him through the material. Carl described it as flat and roundish, sort of like a sand dollar—the sea urchin, and about the same size but with beetle-like wings on its back, and tick-like legs which projected out from beneath its body when it landed, but were otherwise not visible while in flight. He described its flight

In the Shadow of the Ridge 49

as sliding and darting, as if in right angles, and with sudden changes of plane. He used the word *alien*, not as in extraterrestrial, but as in odd or strange. He even said that he was the one to pull it off of Darryl, and that thing was so tenacious that a piece of cloth came away with it.

"I'm getting a bit ahead of myself here, but after Darryl's session, I asked him if he would roll up his pant leg and show me his calf. Sure enough, there were three little scars there. I assume that regardless of how many legs this insect-like critter had, only three of them were dug in deep enough to leave scars. Interestingly enough, Darryl came across as completely indifferent to the marks, saying only that he had no idea how he got them, but didn't doubt that it was connected in some way with being out by the ranch."

"You're right," said Rogers. "I can't say as either one of them mentioned that particular event. What do you make of that? Repressed memory, maybe?"

That was not my guess, and I said as much. "Yes, definitely repressed. But not in the clinical sense. Repression of that sort is usually the result of significant trauma. I don't see that here. I'm thinking there's something else at work; but to be truthful, I haven't had the chance to give it much thought. I'll have to do some research, see what's out there on the subject."

The two of us then went back and forth on possibilities, though more from his end of the phone than mine. Not being critical, but I didn't see much value in supposition—not before doing a little reading first, anyway.

I waited for the opportunity to present itself, and then as tactfully as possible got us back on task by asking if he got the scans I sent him. He said he did, so I brought his attention to the one that Carl did.

"That is, I assume, the entity which he saw while relieving himself out by the trees. When I led him to the recall, I suggested specifically the moment in which, according to Carl, the presence had approached him and was half-squatting and leaning towards him face to face. I then asked him to describe what he was seeing. Let me read from the notes; they're verbatim from the audio:

> It has me by the sides of my head. It's squeezing. I can't move my head. Not hands, something tangling, writhing...constantly feeling as if for a hold. It's eye to eye with me, but I can't fix a stare. Its eyes are flat...wooden...still like speckled stones, but assessing me, contemplating.

"I pushed him at this point to describe the thing, to focus on its facial features. I don't have the audio here at home with me, but if you were to listen to it, you'd hear the frustration in his voice. Here's the verbatim:

> I'm trying, but it won't let me. Maybe its mouth, a sort of puckered hole...ugh...disturbing. A mucous-glazed slit for a nose, like a pussy, a tiny pussy. It won't let me look...What the fuck is that smell? Fucking skunk musk...

"At this point, he starts to snort is the way I describe it, as if he's trying to clear his sinuses. You know, when you have a cold and are stuffed up. He then gags, or chokes something back. It all coincides with what he said during the interview about breathing in mud; I think that's the way he described it."

The other end of the phone had gone quiet, so I thought maybe we had been disconnected. "Still there?" I asked.

"Yeah, yeah—still here," he assured me. "I'm just looking at the drawing. You have it there?"

I said yes, but lied. I had to open up the file. Meanwhile, he was talking.

In the Shadow of the Ridge   51

"So I see the facial features—and he's right, it does sort of look like a pussy positioned over an asshole. I'm not sure how to describe the shape of the head though."

By this time the file had opened and I was looking at it. "Skeletal-like," I suggested. "It has the look of those figures prominent in the petroglyphs and petro-graphs up in the canyons."

"Okay," he said. "I'll go with that. But what's with the body? The main part of it looks like one of those wrapped mummies; you know, where they wrap the legs together with bandage, and the arms across the chest. But what's that other stuff swirling around it?"

To me the part Rogers was referring to looked almost like a school of salmon jumping up into a bit of a water fall. I don't know how else to describe it. "Carl had no explanation for that," I told him.

There was another second of silence, and then Brad asked, "So, the whole thing, real or imagined?"

"Well, let me get to Darryl's session, and then we can go in that direction."

"As interesting or no?"

I picked up the second set of notes. "I'll let you decide."

"Fair enough," he said.

"Similar to Carl, he was receptive to the hypnosis, although not as quick as Carl to go under. I brought him to the moment when the three of them were seated outside the tent and sky watching. His recall of the throat-clearing voice and the object rising up towards and then disappearing over the ridge was consistent with the interview. He, too, then describes the incident with the insect-like creature which attached itself to the back side of his leg. He recalls it moving past his head a number of times, then not being there before he quite suddenly feels something digging into the back of his leg. He reaches back and closes his hand over what he describes as rigid and shell-like, like a large beetle or maybe a crab. He feels it vibrating and then his skin being pierced. He says the thing won't let go, and as he begins to panic, Carl is there pulling the thing off of him. He remembers Carl saying 'what the fuck' and then flipping the thing away with a backhand toss. He hears its wings beating and it goes off towards the ranch.

"From there I move him into the tent. I move him past the incident with the fire, more intent on seeing if he had any recall regarding his calling out. This is where it gets interesting; he describes two different and distinct events. One seems linked to Carl—the calling out, and the other completely independent than anything recalled or even hinted at by Carl. The later of the two is the more prominent in terms of impact, and is therefore the one he recalls first. So that's the way I'll tell it to you, and then we can backtrack.

"According to Darryl, he is awakened. He provides no reason for doing so. However, he says as he does so, he immediately is aware of a figure shimmying its way into the tent from beneath the flap. He wants to yell out, to challenge it, perhaps scare it off. But he finds he has no control whatsoever over his own body. He can't move; he can't yell; he can't do anything. With what he describes as a sort of detached feeling, somewhere between horror and curiosity, he watches this thing, which he describes as vague in form."

I stopped and asked Brad if he had yet to open the file of the second scan I had sent him.

"Give me a second," he said, obviously having not yet done so. "This thing is a little slow tonight; probably the service here in the hotel. Ah, there it is." He then paused a moment. "I see there are two figures here."

"That there is," I confirmed. "The first one—the upper part of the page—is the entity which Carl also saw." I started to make reference to the lower figure with every intent of staying on track

In the Shadow of the Ridge

with the way I sought to tell it, but he cut me off before I could get another word in.

"You think so?" He asked, making no effort to conceal doubt.

Before I could present an argument, he said as if thinking aloud, "I guess I can see it in the body, the shape of it. It's definitely upright—anthropomorphic, but the face is vague; I don't know what to make of those arms?"

At this point, I gave in to Brad's disjointed way of approaching things and willingly went along on the tangent. "I don't think they are meant to be arms. If you remember what Carl described—not just being held aside the head, but by inference by something that was not hands. He said whatever it was was continuously probing as if to secure a better hold. More accurately, I think what we have here are coils, perhaps. If you notice, beside the fact that Darryl has drawn a pair on each side, there is nothing elbow-like, no joints. Not only that—and while I said not to expect Dali, look where the arms are, the coils: well below where you'd expect the shoulders to be. Even a kindergartener drawing a stick figure would include something representative of shoulders and begin the arms there."

Rogers produced a hum of agreement, and then changed his focus to the head and face. "No detail to the face, though. All he included were the eyes, or at least the eye sockets."

"That too," I reminded him, "is a common characteristic of the petroglyphs—round, skull-like, disproportionately large, and otherwise empty. But if you look at the overall perspective of the figure, it suggests he is looking at it from a distance. Carl, on the other hand, had the advantage of being much closer."

"So if I'm getting this right, you are suggesting that Darryl had two encounters of which he was, shall we say, subconscious of at the time. The first one was chronologically parallel to that of Carl..."

Here I abruptly cut him off before he could change the subject, eager to share a theory. "Sorry for interrupting," I prefaced, "but if you recall, Carl said that when he awoke to go and relieve himself, Darryl sat up and said something."

"No fucking way, right?"

"Right. So when Darryl's telling me about this thing under hypnosis, I simply repeated out loud that very line. You know what he said then?"

Of course Brad wouldn't have known. But I did enjoy the moment of heightened drama and expectation.

He played along. "No, what did he say?"

"Basically, he said the thing stepped out of the darkness."

"Materialized?"

I thought for a second before answering, looking for an accurate analogy. "Sort of, but not like Star Trek. I got the impression—and you can listen to the audio yourself when you get it—it was more like coming through a slot. Think like a ticket coming out of the machine at a parking garage. I had asked him if it was like an actor on stage coming through the stage curtain. No curtain, he said, more like a slot. There was no opening, per se. It simply stepped through, and was there."

"That's imaginative," mused Rogers. "And did you get anything more out of him about it?"

I felt an urge at that moment to correct his interpretation of the process, but let it go. Instead I said, "Unfortunately, anyone under hypnosis can only be encouraged to recall what there is to recall. In other words, I don't think there was anything else after that. At least not until he has that second encounter."

He moved on without hesitation, which was something I immediately appreciated in our interaction. I'd call it professionalism—he knew how these things went. "So that brings us to this second drawing here at the bottom."

I asked him how he would describe it.

After a moment's consideration, he said, "Sort of like a caterpillar, but without the segmentation, for a lack of better words."

That, too had been my first impression, and I said as much. I then continued before he could draw me off topic, saying, "And though, again, you can't tell proportions by the drawing, when he was describing it under hypnosis, he said it was easily as long as a man is tall.

"Anyway, the thing slithers into the space between where Carl's sleeping bag is and where he and Mandy are. From its body somewhere, these coils or hose-like structures emerge. As he's lying there, frozen and unable to move or do anything about it, these tubes, what have you, attach to their noses, first to Mandy, and then to his. He's only got his peripheral vision, but he can see that there's one extending in Carl's direction also. The way he described it, it's like the two-finger and thumb position for a bowling ball. Whatever this entity is, it is inserting the ends of these tubes or coils up their nostrils and down their throats. Darryl says that he can't breathe, but there's no sense of panic, as if his senses have been muted or anesthetized. And that's all he remembers."

"Interesting, without a doubt," Brad said after a moment. "I assume you debriefed them both after the sessions."

"That I did, both individually and then together. It was interesting to watch each of their reactions when they heard for the first time what the other had recalled under hypnosis. And I've worked with enough patients and clients to recognize authenticity when I see it. I have no doubt whatsoever that neither expected to hear what they heard. This was no rehearsed act."

"So what do you make of it?" He asked.

I shrugged, although I knew it was an unappreciated gesture, Brad being on the either end of the phone. "I don't have a reliable diagnosis, if you'll excuse the expression. There are documented cases of mass hysteria, if you will. And by mass I mean multiple individuals, and not necessarily a multitude. And there is also the possibility of a collective hallucination, the power of suggestion, as it were.

"Is it possible that they went out there with high expectations and managed to convince themselves to 'see' these things? I guess so. The power of suggestion can be awfully powerful. You get three people of like mind together in an isolated environment; these three people have a shared and collective experience or knowledge in a particular field—in this case the paranormal; there's some sensory stimulation—the lights, the sounds, the smells; and sure, all the elements are there to create the perfect ghost story."

"And would that explain the separate stimuli, the difference in the recall?" he asked. "Would it provide for the difference in the drawings?"

I had to admit it was highly unlikely. "No, that's the part I can't explain."

"So how did you leave it?"

"I am under the impression you'll be hearing from them. Carl, for one seemed to have a concern, but he didn't want to talk about it until he had a chance to sit down with Darryl, and perhaps Mandy, and compare notes, as it were. So that's how we left it."

We spoke for a little while longer after that, most of it peripheral stuff with little or no direct relevance to Carl and Darryl and the sessions. Prior to ending the call, I promised to send Rogers copies of the audio files, and gave him my word I would do my best to write up a report and get it to him within the week. And that's how we left that at that particular time.

When I went out to the parlor—the living room others might call it, Jess was watching television and had a mug of beer, half of which had already been drained. Noticing me, which she did with a bit of frown, she said, "I poured one for you too, but that was almost an hour ago."

In the Shadow of the Ridge 57

I looked first at the mug to which she had gestured, and then to the clock over the mantle. It was after 9:00. "I'm sorry," I said. "I hadn't expected to take so long."

Of course, she had only been playing with me. She knew how I got when talking about my cases. "That's why I went with the Hacker-Pschorr," she said with an impish grin. "I know you like to let it get to room temperature, anyway."

Indicating her mug, I quipped, "So I see you're not partial one way or the other."

"Actually, if you want to know, I let it sit waiting for you. But when the big hand got past the six, I decided I had been patient enough. But yes, it was still chilled then."

I sat in my chair. "Well, let me catch up and maybe we can split another."

"And you can tell me about your friend Brad and what kept you so deeply in conversation."

With some 50s movie as the background, I filled her in. She was more than just politely interested, and even had some questions and comments which were quite poignant from an outside perspective. Particularly was a certain similarity between this case and the one with Samantha Wilkins.

"It just seems to me," she said, "that it's more than a coincidence the way they both describe how the presence came and went. Not so much that they say the same thing, but that they both—meaning the two separate cases—go out of the way to convey something other than a visible or measurable opening. It's not a door; it's not a curtain; it's not a void. And at the same time, it is not what you would call a materialization."

By this time, we were both working on that third bottle of beer we were sharing, and I for one had that warm glow which comes from just the right amount of alcohol stimulation.

"See, that's why I married you. It's all in the details."

"I'm sure it would have come to you," she said being modest.

"I'm sure it would have, just not so quickly."

It was about two weeks later, perhaps fifteen days, that I received a brief email from Brad Rogers. The message informed me that both Carl and Darryl had undergone the MRI process, and that the preliminary results were negative. Despite the results, at least from what I inferred, both continue to insist they had been implanted that night with some sort of organic transmitter or router, if you will, which continues to allow some other-worldly or alien entity to read and know their thoughts and to study them from the inside out.

Our communication after that point began to fall off, much in the way that occurs between people brought together by particular incidents or narrow interests. But that again would have cause to change.

AUTUMN, 2013

It wasn't until October of 2013 that the Skinwalker Ranch came prominently back into my life. Not that it hadn't been on the radar or I had been completely ignoring the place. That wasn't possible. Not only had I continued to "authenticate" subjects on behalf of Brad Rogers and his organization—a handful of which had some connection to the ranch and surrounding area, but my wife had become in the interim the local expert on the paranormal, and in general the go-to person for the locals whenever there was something unexplainable amiss. Which here in the middle, almost literally, of so much surrounding reservation land—the Uintah-Ouray, to be exact—was fairly routine. The Ute have their superstitions and lore.

Not too far south from where we are is Fort Duchesne, and somewhat further south of that is Randlett. Both towns are actually census-designated places, meaning they are not formally incorporated and with borders which are, shall we say, less than clearly delineated. In this case, both are on or bordered by reservation land, and the residents are more than 90% Ute.

A few years back, we started hearing stories of a dog-man roaming the neighborhoods in those two areas during the nighttime hours. The locals claimed hearing something walking across their roofs. The common report was that whenever anyone went out to investigate, this dog-man would make its escape by leaping from that roof to the one of the next door neighbor, and then disappearing into the darkness. The catch, of course, was that the houses are routinely separated by thirty feet or more; which would suggest more flying than leaping.

While most of these encounters were pretty much the same, there was one in particular in which a homeowner down in Randlett claims to have come face to face with the creature. From the way he tells it, he heard a noise outside. Grabbed his shotgun. Went out the back door and around to the side of the house where he heard the noise. As he rounded the house, he saw a figure rise up from the other side of a tank of sorts that was there. He swears the creature was no more than a few yards from him. He says it was as tall as a man, stood upright, was covered with long, scraggly hair which looked black in the darkness, and had the limbs of a canine, but more proportionate to those of a human. The hands, which he said were positioned kangaroo-like out front, were more paw-like, but with what appeared to be longish claws or nails. To him, the creature had a somewhat emaciated appearance and gave off an offensive odor, somewhere between something which has been dead for a while and a feral musk. The sight of the thing caused him to freeze, and by the time he thought to lift the gun, the critter bounded off into the dark towards some olive trees clustered at the base of the hills to the back of his neighbor's house. The distance, he estimates, was a couple of hundred feet, which the dog-man covered in mere seconds. He described the critter's gait as awkward and abnormal but incredibly quick.

None of these stories were featured in the *Deseret*, but Jessica had her sources. Like I said, she had become the local expert; which in and of itself is fairly interesting considering she is not Native American. But since Vernal is relatively speaking a small place, everyone kind of gets to know everyone else, even if intrusiveness is avoided as a rule.

With Jessica, the interest in the local paranormal began with that coin. Well, not really the coin, but the individual who brought it to her. There's another store owner she met through one of those civil association meetings in which business owners and other influential people, both local and in the outlying area, get together to discuss the current state of affairs and brainstorm strategies for growing the common cause. The woman ran a place called Gitana's in Lapoint, which is another one of those unincorporated

In the Shadow of the Ridge

communities. It too incorporates reservation land—the Uintah-Ouray.

According to my wife, the two of them got to talking, as another individual in attendance had introduced them given the similarities to the two stores. Although I have never been down to Gitana's, Jessica tells me it's more of a general store, but that Bonnie—she's the owner—is both Native American—Ute—and the daughter of a tribal shaman, which is another word for witchdoctor.

"She doesn't sell much that is related to the topic, but she routinely dispenses information and gives counsel," is the way Jessica explained it.

According to Bonnie, once their conversation got around to the topic, the Indian who came into her shop is what she called a shadow walker. Jessica's description was significantly more elaborate, but I'll summarize by saying he is supposedly this ancient entity, perhaps thousands of years old, who exists on different planes. The Native Americans out here are big on the concept of planes—and I say that with all due respect—and their connection to the life beyond. He's called a shadow walker because he supposedly uses shadows as portals, or at least the portals he uses are concealed in or by shadow.

Apparently, this ancient Indian, who is sometimes seen with a younger Indian, has been part of the local lore for generations upon generations. The fact that his description and appearance has not varied over all that time, at least to me, kind of lends the whole thing a sort of Santa Claus vibe, but who am I to dismiss local lore?

Anyway, one thing led to another—and we're talking at least five years at that point, and Jessica had gotten into the whole skin walker thing. Her shop was routinely stocked with turquoise trinkets, locally made totems, corn pollen, corn silk, local cedar, creator pipes, and even sweet grass—all things used to ward off and protect against, well, skin walkers.

I'll also add that Vernal sitting only a stone's throw from the mythical path of the Skinwalker didn't hurt business any, especially now that people who wanted these items had a place to go for them.

For the benefit of those not so well acquainted, this mythical path is a ridge of rock which runs north to south. It includes along the way local places such as Lapoint, Fort Duchesne, and Randlett; the entire length of which has an elevation of anywhere from 4800 feet to more than a mile. The ridge simply adds to that. And, of course, right in the middle of it all sits the ranch property

So where is this all going? You ask.

Trust me, we're getting there.

The Native Americans living on and around the reservation associate the ranch property with this particular extent of the ridge. It's actually called Skinwalker Ridge. The actual reference goes back to the early 1800s, and coincides with the arrival of the White man—although the concept of skin walkers—and I don't mean to sound pedantic—goes back well beyond that, literally thousands of years.

In the more recent manifestation, the Ute believe the Navajo witchdoctors called upon spirits from the beyond, a spiritual world, to seek vengeance upon them for perceived wrongs. From my perspective, these wrongs were more than just perceived. If history tells it accurately, the Ute sided with White soldiers to drive the Navajo from the Great Basin, raiding their villages to kill the men, steal the livestock and horses, and then sell the women and children into slavery to the Apache and Mexicans further down south.

In a sort of turn-around is fair play scenario, the Ute themselves were then driven from the Great Basin, and on the way, they were tormented and worse by this entity which would come out of the canyons, do its thing, and then disappear again without a trace. They referred to this entity as a Skinwalker, but with a different

In the Shadow of the Ridge 63

connotation than that of the traditional sense. This one was darker and clearly supernatural.

Up to that point, skin walker was a term given to tribal members who camouflaged themselves in animal skins, primarily coyote and bison, in order to sneak up closely to Ute villages to do recognizance and prepare against attack. Since then the notion of what a skin walker is has changed a bit, but the concept of torment and victimization remains pretty much the same. Regardless, to this day, the Ute believe the Skinwalker—the supernatural one—yet roams that particular stretch of the ridge, and that its lair is there above the ranch. Therefore, that whole area is taboo. The Ute don't go there, and they won't permit anyone else to either.

Not that I have done so myself—Jessica has, but those who have had the opportunity to discuss the topic of the ranch with the Native Americans hereabout, come away with a sort of mixed bag in which both the paranormal and the extraterrestrial are thrown in together. In fact, any conversation about the ranch, and depending on who you talk to, refers to the place as either the UFO ranch or Skinwalker Ranch, and at times even interchangeably.

There are some constants though. For example, those who go with the UFO name are more likely to bring up extraterrestrial and ET experiences, the most common being unidentified flying objects. Personally, I get the biggest kick out of those people who talk about seeing truck-sized and even football field sized craft passing overhead, all aglow and with flashing lights of different colors. Personally, I would think that if something like that was happening, there'd be a whole bunch more people talking about it, and from a lot more places than just around here. But for the moment I'm going to reserve comment.

As for the Skinwalker disciples, their take is decidedly towards the paranormal and supernatural. They're the ones who talk about portals, alternate dimensions, light anomalies, and entities with the ability to move in and out of our world, as it were. Any encounter seems to fall within the poltergeist or haunted house phenomenon, including ghostly figures, moving objects, things that go bump in the night, sounds without sources of origin, and unexplained occurrences and behaviors.

The case of Lena Bishop falls into this category, but with some other elements which even a professional "skeptic" such as myself would have difficulty discounting or chalking up to individual idiosyncrasies.

I had no way of knowing at the time, or any reason to suspect, that the new case Rogers had called me about involved a local individual with whom I had passing familiarity. He has this thing for confidentiality, and rightfully so. Even with Carl and Darryl, I had only their first names to go by until they arrived at my office. And while I had not actually met the woman, Jessica had, and they had developed a bit of a store owner-customer relationship.

I can't pin it down to an exact date, or even a general one at that, when Jessica first brought Lena up in conversation. It was, though, quite some time ago, a year at least. And even then, I'd have to assume there had been significant interaction between them prior to give Jessica reason to consider it intimately worthy of our beer ritual.

I'm encapsulating here, but go with me.

I remember her saying to me—I'll assume it was seated before the TV, "There's this local woman who has been coming in fairly routinely, and we got to talking."

"About what?"

"Up until today, she's been cautious, kind of prefacing her questions about the different items in the store, as if she wanted to give the impression it was just an interest. But she always buys something, usually a spirit ward of some sort."

"You mean something to ward off evil spirits, demons, that kind of ward?"

In the Shadow of the Ridge 65

"Yeah," she smiled with a shrug. "I don't know why I said it that way."

"But today was different?"

She was accustomed to my prompting, but couldn't resist. "Always the psychologist; I'm getting to it. Today she seemed upset, or maybe distracted is a better word. It took a little probing on my part, but eventually I got her to talk, or maybe she was just at that point. She starts telling me that there is something going on at her home, something not normal. Not natural, was the way she put it.

"At first I wasn't sure how to take her. People come into the store all the time talking about chasing away things they can't see but can feel, or who swear they are being targeted by a Skinwalker. Just yesterday, a guy came in and bought a snake skin totem—any Ute or Navajo knows it doesn't work like that, a creator's pipe, and a thing of the sweet grass. He said he wasn't paying no Shaman $200 to smudge his house; he was going to do it himself.

"But I could see in her eyes that she was really stressed. I knew there was nothing in the store which I could sell her that would make a difference, and I didn't really want to get into the specifics of her problem. For all I knew, she was a deeply troubled individual, and up until then had been keeping it in check. I really didn't have much to go on, other than the other times she was in the store. And even then our conversation was the usual small talk, that and what I could tell her about the various items she was interested in. I didn't know what else to do, so I recommended she go see Bonnie."

I don't remember anything else which stands out about that particular conversation, but sometime after, six months, maybe more, Jessica brought her up again. Apparently she had gone through a rough patch and had been hospitalized for period of time. She didn't go into detail, and I didn't ask.

"She looked tired and older," said Jess. "But other than telling me about the rough patch, she didn't bring up anything about the house. She did, however, buy a small turquoise amulet—a nice oval-shaped stone set in silver—to give to her youngest daughter. She played it off as her daughter having a thing for turquoise, but I could see it was something more."

"Do you even know this woman's name?" I asked her. "I don't recall you ever mentioning it."

"Haven't I? Lena," she said. "I don't remember her ever telling me her last name, but she frequently uses her credit card. It's Bishop, I believe."

"Just curious," I told her. "It helps visualize when there's a name to go with a story." And that was the last I had heard of Lena Bishop until Brad Rogers called.

That call came towards the end of office hours on October 12, 2013, and had been prefaced by a sequence of emails. After the usual exchange of pleasantries, Rogers told me he had confirmed the case, and that it was definitely for me if I was interested. He filled me in on some of the surface details, explaining along the way that this one had come to him through the usual channels, but had the kind of complex layers you come across once in a lifetime.

The subject, he said, was a woman, early to mid-forties, married and with three children, the oldest of which was 20 and the youngest of which had just turned 10. Both were daughters. The middle child, a boy, was 15. The subject's husband is Ute, as is she. This is her second marriage. She was currently residing in Vernal—about two years now, but had previously been living in Lapoint. That's where the incidents took place. He said he had checked out the house and the property, and in his professional opinion, he thinks there's something to the subject's claims.

When I pressed a little, he acknowledged that it was a paranormal thing. "She's convinced," he said, "that she went through a portal, into some other dimension or plane, and when she came out, well, everything was changed, if only subtly. But she could sense it then, and even so more now. But there's more to it.

In the Shadow of the Ridge 67

She says her two daughters were with her at the time, but that she and the older daughter, from what she says, had a different experience than the younger daughter, who for the sake of description, may have remained behind. She's not clear on the point."

I tried to interrupt him here, but he asked me to be patient, stopping me before I could say or ask anything.

Continuing, he said, "No doubt, you were going to ask about how a car goes through a portal, or something. But I think it's best that I don't give you any real details. Regardless, that's all incidental. They key here is that the subject believes that her younger daughter, the one who may or may not have gone through this portal, has somehow been changed. There's more to it than that; any way, that's where you come in. I'm convinced after meeting with her that she has suppressed recall of that particular event—and by extension others. We hope you'll have the same success you had with Carl and Darryl."

"Did you get a chance to speak with the daughter?" I asked, just out of curiosity.

"No," he said. "The subject doesn't want to go in that direction at the moment. But she didn't rule it out. Perhaps that's something you can suggest, if you get that far."

"And she's willing to meet with me?"

"Apparently she is somewhat familiar with you. She's been at your wife's store. At first, she appeared somewhat hesitant. But when I assured her of full confidentiality, and that the network would take care of the financial end of things, she said she'd give it a try. Besides, it seems to me that she really needs to get this thing resolved."

"What's the name?" I asked.

"Her name is Lena Bishop. When can I tell her to come in?"

Of course, I immediately recognized the name, and then had a passing thought to call Jessica. But I suppressed the notion, and gave my attention to the task, instead.

I gave a quick look to my schedule. "Monday. What is that, the 15th? Yeah, Monday would be fine. 10:00."

"Fine," he said. "I'll tell her. And Wade, we're going to stay in close contact on this one."

THE DREAM HOUSE

Lena Bishop, her husband, and their three children had been living in a small rented house south of 121 in Lapoint. For Lena it was her first marriage. Her daughter, Maggie, at the time just 14, was the product of a previous relationship but not a marriage. (Brad was incorrect on this point.) She and Drew—he was not Native American, Maggie's father, met when they were both working in a local variety store. She was nineteen going on 20 at the time, and a year or so out of high school. She had been telling herself she would continue on to college, but she knew, too, that it was just words. Drew had just turned 21. She had Maggie a little less than a year later, and less than a year after that, Drew was gone. It was an amicable parting, as there was little between them to hold on to.

She had known Wayne Bishop most of her life—they both grew up on the reservation and were practically neighbors—but could not recall ever having any sort of interest in him when it came to physical attraction or the idea of a relationship. First of all, he was a couple of years younger than her, and to be truthful, she really didn't find him all that attractive. She couldn't even explain adequately what it was that grew between them or how. Nevertheless, he was a good man and had a career, one that paid well and had some cache. They were married in 1998. She was at the time already pregnant with their son Aaron. Emma, the youngest, came along in 2004. Lena was a stay-at-home mom.

In late October of 2008, Wayne brought home news of a bank-owned house which a friend told him was about to come on the market, and that if they were interested, he had an in if they wanted to make an offer. In fact, he knew the price that would get it done, although the real estate handling the sale was going to start with a significantly higher asking price.

When Wayne told Lena what the get-it-done price was, she asked him as to the catch. It seemed low given what he told her about the place.

"I drove by to take a look on the way home. Other than being in the middle of no-place," he said, "it's gorgeous—at least from the outside."

"There's got to be a catch," repeated Lena.

Wayne just shook his head. "From what Greg says, and this from his brother-in-law—he's got some big position in the bank, the previous owner just up and left. Apparently there were financial issues."

So together Lena and Wayne went that weekend to look at the house, walking about the property and peering through windows.

Liking what she saw, Lena asked, "Can we afford it?"

"If we can get it at the price Greg says, then yeah. It'll be a little tight; but definitely doable."

So they did it; the bought the house of their dreams.

They moved in the last week of December, and right after the Christmas holiday.

As for the actual property—and I've walked it myself, it is located north of 121 and Deep Creek, up on the east side of Mountain Road. There's a neighbor to the south and on the same side of the road, but there's a rise which separates the two properties. There is another neighbor on the west side of the road, and then a short walk to the south. Other than that, there's little to nothing else up that way. And once you get past the Bishop property, the road just continues north and west, unpaved and snaking its way through the rocks and hills off into a whole bunch of nothingness.

Size-wise, the property is just short of ten acres, most of which are to the back of the house and straight up onto the ridge. The only flat ground surrounds the house. There is a wrap-around driveway out front which is separated from the house by a fence, a few steps up, and a carpet of green lawn. There is a second driveway to the south which leads to a connected garage and a large paved parking area capable of fitting multiple vehicles with room to spare. In addition, at the back of the house there is a deck, four large trees beyond, and then plenty of yard for the kids to play in before you come to a fence which runs along the base of the ridge. Just to the other side of the fence, the terrain immediately turns into two twin hills of dirt, rock, and some scrub brush. And while we're not talking mountainous heights, they're definitely three or four stories up, and climb at a pretty steep angle. That climb leads up to the ridge, which then goes on for as far as the eyes can see to the north, broken up only by the Lapoint reservoir about a mile from the house. To the east is Deep Creek Road. All in all, it is an isolated location, somewhat breathtaking in its own way, but graveyard quiet and still.

The house itself is contemporary, built sometime around 2000. Style-wise, it is a low ranch with two extensions running out towards the front and separated by a recessed entrance, and one extension to the back. There is an attached garage to the south side of the house, out in front of which is a large multi-car driveway and parking area. There is an additional detached garage-like structure to the east end of the drive, off the back of which runs a fence which turns in towards the yard, and combined with the property fence, creates a sweeping and unpaved drive to the back of the house and beyond the deck and tree-shaded yard. To the north of the house, there is another fence which runs from the front curb, all the way to the hills, where it joins the back extent, thereby closing in that part of the property. There is an additional garage/storage structure to the back of the house to the north, access to which is unpaved, and outside of the fence, but abutting it and at its rear the hill. To access the greater part of the property, which includes the hills and an extent of the ridge itself, you have to circumvent the fence to the south, and then make the climb up.

72   **In the Shadow of the Ridge**

At this point, and before I go any further, let me preface that all data was collected during our sessions, of which there were three different kinds: the pre-conference, the hypnosis, and a post conference, or debriefing. Without getting too deeply into the clinical side of it, once Lena made clear her suspicions about her daughter and how convinced she was as to the portal event, my objective became to mine for the kind of detail which would only surface through assisted recall. Basically, I was looking to surface the kind of details which would reveal a pattern to some premeditated and intelligent behavior evidencing the presence of a paranormal or alien entity or force. Having said that, I realize how ridiculous it sounds. But I'm not so sure that'll still be the case when all is said and done.

Lena says that there were absolutely no issues for the first few months they were in the home. However, that was to change towards the end of March in 2009. Up until that point, mainly due to the snow, she and Wayne didn't have much in the way of opportunity to explore any part of the property which was less than immediately accessible, or for that matter did they have any real inclination to do so.

From what she recalls, she was in the house with the three kids and the family dog, a collie-Shepard mix, named, of all things, Tonto. The fact that Wayne was home, and running about the property in an all-terrain vehicle he had got for himself as a sort of belated Christmas present, led her to believe it was a Saturday, but definitely a weekend.

She says he had only been out there maybe 30 minutes at the most. She remembers most distinctly the sound of the ATV fading as Wayne made his way out around the back fence and up into the hills leading onto the ridge. After that, with the television on and the kids running about the house, she only caught short coughs of the engine.

The next thing she knows, he's in the kitchen and hurrying her to put on her boots and coat. "There's something you've got see," he keeps repeating, obviously worked up and excited.

His only response when she asks what it is, is to pull her along and say she has to see it for herself, but that if she doesn't hurry, it'll get away.

They only had the one ATV at the time, so she climbs in behind him and holds on for dear life as he speeds up what barely passes for a trail. Once up the hill, they bump along at a pace she describes as less than cautious, heading towards an area upon the ridge which is speckled with monolith-like rock formations, some of which are grouped together and others standing off on their own.

Wayne maneuvers the ATV through a sort of mini-canyon which passes first this way and then that through a series of these formations rising 12 to 15 feet over head, and about half as long and as far around as their house. He goes about a hundred feet in, comes to a stop, and turns off the engine.

"I saw it lope off into here," he said, using an extended arm and hand to suggest a vague direction ahead of them.

"What are you talking about?" Lena asks him. Then somewhat impatiently, she adds that the kids are alone in the house.

Wayne gives her that look she has become accustomed to when he thinks she's stressing over nothing, and then reminds her that Maggie is 14, not four.

"I'm not sure I can describe it," he said.

And just then, Lena let out a gasp and an involuntary squeal.

As she catches her breath, she manages to squeak out, "Over there", while pointing to a recess between the rocks to their left.

"That's it," says Wayne in a harsh whisper and grabbing on to her outstretched arm.

Lena described what she saw as canine-like. Like a wolf, but definitely not a wolf, she said. When encouraged to go on, she indicated it was big like a wolf, meaning much bigger than the coyotes common to the area. But though it had a wolf-like aspect, it didn't move like a wolf, or carry itself as she thought a wolf might. Not only that, but it was abnormal looking in a way she couldn't quite pin down with the right words, other than to say it looked out of proportion, as if thrown together from spare parts. She recalled it was covered with black hair which appeared in spots matted, and in others longer and thinner. Like a balding guy's comb-over is how she put it.

When they first spotted it, it kind of froze, staying back in the shadow of the rock, but was clearly making eye contact. The eyes, she said, were pale and an opaque or clouded blue in color, and eerily intelligent. But as soon as Wayne made a move to get off the ATV, it turned and moved deeper into the rock.

When it again appeared, it was on the other side of the rocks to their right and at the top of the formation, easily 12 to 15 feet above their heads. Again, she saw it before Wayne did; he had gone over to the place in the rock where it had been.

"Up there," she remembers saying, Wayne's eyes following the line of her pointing finger.

"Hey, what the…" he said, and again in a harsh whisper, as if he couldn't believe his own eyes.

She said there's no way it could have gotten up there without them seeing it. There was just too much open space. She then called Wayne ridiculous for suggesting there had to be an underground tunnel, or something similar, and that it simply went beneath them and came out on the other side.

I refocused her and asked her to follow the wolf. She became hesitant, and it took some coaxing on my part to get her to continue.

She said it sat there atop the rock, squatting and hunched over not like a dog, but like a monkey, back on its haunches and its front limbs down to each side, and almost as if smiling. She noted that there in the light, she saw it had a dog-like snout, but not as long or as pronounced. Its ears too were canine, but longer and sticking out more than a dog's would. Wayne, she could see out of the corner of her eye, was fumbling about in his coat for his cellphone, and just as he raised it to snap a photo, the creature spun and vaulted to the back of the rock and was again gone from sight.

Frightened, she pleaded for Wayne to take her back to the house. Initially he ignored her and started to head after the creature. But she called out his name and made him come back. Together they got back on the ATV and turned it around. No sooner did they get the vehicle back in motion, the animal sauntered upright into the middle of their path, but a good 50 feet ahead of them. She had assumed that Wayne would stop, but instead he accelerated. The creature responded by leaping off towards a lone rock formation, a little more than man height and no wider around than a kitchen table. Wayne steered the ATV right at it, but when they got there, there was no sign of the thing, and no way for it to have run out onto the ridge without them seeing it. There was just no place for it to hide; yet, it had disappeared.

Shortly after the encounter, Lena started having what she called her waking dreams or waking nightmares. She wasn't certain in her recall, whether under hypnosis or in our regular sessions, exactly when these began, but she was confident in saying within a day or two of that encounter. These episodes continued for a number of months and without pattern, and then suddenly stopped. She states that she only once mentioned them to Wayne, and to no one else, and even then only briefly. She didn't provide a reason, only saying that at the time, when she did think about it, it didn't seem all that important. When she did first tell Wayne, he chalked it up to the encounter up on the ridge and the stress of being in a new house.

According to Lena, the first time it happened, she had gone into bed at the usual time. Wayne, as was his routine, came in a while after, staying out in the family room to watch the end of his program. She remembers checking the clock. It was a few minutes before eleven. From what she recalls—and it was in pretty impressive detail, she was dreaming, the usual oddly sequenced and surrealistic events which occur in dreams, and suddenly she is staring at what she adamantly identifies as a werewolf.

To her what stands out the most is she was quite aware, even at the time, of which part of it was dream, and which part was werewolf. To her, the dream sequence was the dream sequence, and she accepted it as much. But the werewolf part was something else altogether, and from what she says, real.

That first time, she says, the werewolf was standing inside the room and beside the window of the bedroom to the north side of the house. When pressed on the matter, and by pressed I mean encouraged to elaborate, she described it as just standing there as still as a statue. And despite the relative darkness of the room, she could make out some of its features. There was, according to her, a kind of aura to it outlining its shape and giving it dimension. Its eyes were dark, she said, but at the same time visible. Of course, by the time she realized she was sitting up and awake, her pulse quickened and her breaths short and harsh, there was nothing there but the window. Wayne never stirred; and that too was to become part of the pattern. It was, she said, as if he was under some sort of spell, body always rigid and breathing shallow. She was never alarmed by it.

These sort of psychosomatic encounters then started to occur more frequently, and always at night; although Lena did suggest she was aware at times during the day of a lingering presence. Regardless, there was an apparent pattern to the events, and this consistent with that first stage of deep sleep. Invariably, the werewolf would be there, at first always near to the window, and sometimes, although the vertical blinds were closed at night, clearly visible to her just outside the window. By the time she had experienced its presence a half-dozen times or so, and this she estimated over a period of 10 days, perhaps two weeks, it seemed to her that there were two significant developments. The first was her ability to sustain awareness of the werewolf's presence, if only for fractions of a second longer. The second was that the werewolf had become emboldened. It began to come deeper into the room, first standing at the end of their bed, and then there at her side of the bed and within arm reach. Not once, however, did it ever reach towards her, seemingly content to stare. Prior to its last visit, as she put it, she recalls waking to find it entering from the hallway, and she realizing the way people do in dreams that it had been in her children's rooms. After that, she recalls its presence only one more time, and that in proximity to the window, but with its back turned. She did not in her remaining time there living in the house experience similar waking dreams.

As I did with Carl and Darryl, while under hypnosis—and this on multiple occasions, I asked her to draw the werewolf. She, however, each time simply said she couldn't do it and made no effort to even try. There was no adamancy about her actions, nor did I perceive her as intentionally objectionable or contrary. In my professional opinion, she was incapable of complying with the request; either due to some psychological block or some unexplained physical interference. After that, I did not again attempt to get her to draw.

Oddly enough, though, she had no trouble describing it verbally, as if she was at the very moment looking right at it. While the detail was overall general, she stated that the face, as she recalls, was reminiscent more of a man than a wolf, with a nose which was broad and flat, but nothing like the snout of a canine. She did say it had a "wolfish" grin, but there was no humor to it. There was hair on the face, most prominently, she recalls, down the bridge of the nose and flowing along the cheeks towards the ears. She described it as smooth, as if "brushed", and she believed black in color. She repeated that the eyes were dark, but visible, and that the ears were coyote-like, only shorter and more pointed, and towards the top of the head, more so than down on the side like we have. The height of the man-wolf she derived from the window itself, saying only that he wasn't as tall. She described his frame as thin, and his presence as curious more than threatening, although she herself always felt something ominous about it.

During the debriefing session after which she first told me about the werewolf, I explained to her that as a psychologist I have some knowledge of the physiological process associated with dreaming. I then explained the association between REM and deep sleep, and added that the first dream stage usually takes place about 90 minutes after falling asleep, which would account for the 12:30 hour she remembered. Continuing at the risk of sounding too doctor-like, I told her that it is towards the later part of this first stage that we are most aware that we are dreaming, and it is these details we are most likely to recall. Seeing a werewolf-like specter, given her encounter with the canine creature only a day or two before, therefore seemed reasonable. Dreams are, after all, I told her, the brain's means of defragmenting all the data we receive on a daily basis, and then finding a way to categorize and store it all according to previous experiences.

Lena was very patient with me, but it was also quite obvious she wasn't buying it.

She agreed with me, but then told me about the footprints outside the bedroom window and other areas about the house, and the others she and Wayne found leading towards the back of the garage and up to the ridge. All identical, she insisted, and made seemingly by the same creature.

In later sessions of hypnosis, I made some effort to surface recall which would provide for these footprints, but as she didn't actually see them being made—well, you can only pull from the subconscious things that are actually there. She did, however, email me photos she and Wayne had taken. I admit the prints did have a canine semblance to them, but size in terms of proportionality did not fit a presence the size she described. My take on it was that they were in all likelihood coyote prints. Although, admittedly, the presence of coyotes did not adequately explain Lena's claims.

IT'S NOT THE TELEVISION

The departure of the waking dreams was not the end of it all, but according to Lena, just the next step in what was to become an escalation of paranormal activity.

She wasn't sure of an exact date, only that it was late April or early May, but she recalls walking about the property with Emma, who at the time was four. They started out innocently enough, tracing the white brick path extending off the rear deck and out into the property, stopping along the way to look at how nicely the grass was filling in while Emma ran over to hug the trees. From there, they made their way out past the fence running along the base of the ridge and headed over towards the garage. She and Wayne had been giving some consideration to putting in a paved driveway, and she wanted to get a casual look at the length. Suddenly, as they moved out past the back of the garage, Emma, who was walking a few steps ahead, darted away in the direction of the scattering of rock formations which sat a short way up the sloping terrain. She ran into the middle of them, and then turned and ran back out, where she stood waving her mother over.

When Lena, who was in no hurry, managed to catch up, she said, "Do you like these rocks, Emma?"

Emma responded by pointing and saying, and in a tone that was as matter-of-fact as could be, "This is the poor hole, Mommy."

Lena recalls smiling, and then asking with a mother's patience, "What's so poor about it, honey?"

By the expression on her daughter's face, she knew, however, what she was saying and what she meant to say were two different things.

"Oh, Mommy," she giggled. "This is where they come out."

Lena acknowledges that at the moment she wasn't putting two and two together. "Who comes out, Emma?" She asked. She then recalled looking over at the rocks as is she half-expected someone to be there.

Emma gave a little shrug and with little or no affectation, answered, "Everything." After which she simply turned and skipped off, completely oblivious to what she had just said, and her attention to something else that had caught her eye.

Later on when she had time to think about it, Lena came to the conclusion that Emma meant to say 'portal'. How she would know that word, or to use it in that way, however, remained the question.

With a little guidance on my part, she suggested that Aaron was a potential source. He was a video game enthusiast, and had a small collection of graphic novels, most of which were science fiction.

Within a couple of days after the backyard incident, the poltergeist activity started. Lena referred to it as the accommodation period. To her, it was as if the family was being visited by different entities looking for the ideal match.

At first, she stated, it was nothing all that noticeable. Just kind of double-take stuff, or where you stop and consider, like open drawers in the kitchen, or lamps on in the family room—things like that.

But then, she said, it just started becoming all too frequent and noticeable for there not to be something to it.

"It was literally," she said, "like something out of all those paranormal and horror movies. I'd come into the kitchen and all of the draws and cabinet doors would be open. One time, I came in to find all of the forks taken out of the utensil draw and lined up parallel one to the other across the top of the counter. And I mean they were perfect. It would have taken a person, I don't know, five or ten minutes to do it, between taking out all the forks and then making sure they were so exactly even and in line like that. And there would have been some noise. You can't even open that draw without rattling things around. It completely freaked me out.

"I ran out of the kitchen to get my cellphone, which was in my bag on top of the dresser in my bedroom. When I got back, it was as if I had imagined the whole thing. There wasn't a fork in sight; everything was back in the drawer.

"Now, if it was just me, I'd have thought I was losing my mind. But it wasn't. Wayne actually found his tooth brush in the glove compartment of his truck. He thought Aaron or Maggie was pranking him. Both denied it; and what was even more interesting—at least I thought so—is that they didn't blame each other. Instead, I saw them exchange glances as if sharing something between them.

"And like I said, things like this were happening all the time. We found shoes lined up in the bathtub. We'd be watching television and it would just turn itself off. Wayne got up in the middle of the night one time and all the lights were on in the house. Maggie, who almost never makes her bed, unless I'm giving her stress about it, came home from school to find it made. She came out to the kitchen where I was doing whatever, and at the same time thanked me and apologized for forgetting. But I know I didn't make it.

"There's so much more," she said. "I could fill up a book with it."

When I asked her if she was afraid, or if she had considered doing something about it, she answered that she eventually sought the advice of a friend of hers who owned a local grocery and variety store near Fort Duchesne. That was Bonnie from Gitana's.

According to Lena, Bonnie—who many of the locals believe to be a spiritual conduit or some type of link to other planes—arranged for her grandfather, a tribal Shaman, to come to the house where he performed a traditional Ute ritual to rid the house of spirits. She added that she convinced him to walk out to the rock formation which Emma had called the portal, but that when they got out there, he refused to approach it and then warned Lena to stay away from the area, and to keep her children away from it, too. When she tried to tease more information from him, telling him what

In the Shadow of the Ridge

Emma had said, his expression grew concerned, and then he simply repeated the warning about avoiding the spot and not going up on the ridge.

Regardless, the poltergeist activity fell off after that, with only an occasional incident here and there and with little to no impact.

Shortly after that, stage two started. To Lena, it was as if stronger entities had made claim to the family and house, and in the process had chased or scared off the poltergeist and less powerful spirits or ghosts.

She recalls it was late morning and she was in the laundry room ironing some of Wayne's shirts. Casually humming, she stopped, having become suddenly aware of low voices and giggling. But she knew she was the only one in the house. Maggie and Aaron were in school. Emma was in daycare. And, of course, Wayne was at work. Her first thought was the television, which she herself had not had on, but which Maggie or Aaron routinely watched in their own rooms while getting dressed for school and might have forgotten to turn off. The kids' rooms to the other side of the house, perhaps, she thought, she just hadn't noticed until then.

She finished the shirt she was working on, put it on a hanger, and went to have a look. However, as she made her way down the narrow hallway, there was no indication of any sound. Going first into Maggie's room, the door of which was mostly closed, she found the television off. As she turned to leave, she again heard the voices, after which there was a moment of silence, and then the same type of giggling. She stopped in her tracks, listening to find the direction. But it again had gone quiet. Feeling silly about it, she checked Maggie's closet, and then even took a look beneath the bed. Of course, there was nothing there. She left the room and closed the door behind her, standing in the hall between closed doors and her head atilt. Again came the voices, followed by a moment of silence, and then the giggling, and all remote as if there in the house, but at the same time not there in the house.

Stepping softly, she moved to Aaron's room—television off, and then to Emma's, and each time conducted her search. There was nothing under either bed, and nothing in either closet. Closing the door as she left Emma's room, she again heard the voices and giggling, and this time was convinced it was coming from the family room. When she got there, prepared to confront whoever it was, she instead was surprised to find that the sound was coming from the small surround sound speakers affixed to the wall brackets either side of the entertainment system. And while the voices had a metallic quality to the tone, they were clearly not amplified in the electronic sense. Instead, it reminded her of the tin can telephones her father made for her and her brother when they were kids, the kind with the string connecting the two cans together—only her father had used some phone wire he had lying about.

At that point, she was somewhat relieved, thinking that the system was somehow picking up a signal bouncing around the rock of the ridge and manifesting it as sound. Being a Ute, however, she also said a simple prayer and then as politely as possible asked any spirits present to please leave. Whether or not that was the reason, she heard no more voices that day.

She acknowledged that she didn't mention the incident to Wayne or the children. She also said she could think of no reason why she didn't, or any reason why she should have.

That next morning, while having breakfast, Maggie told her that she had heard Aaron talking in his sleep—at least she assumed he was asleep.

"I couldn't really hear what he was saying," she said. "But then it'd go all quiet again, so that I thought he'd gone back to sleep. And then he'd start laughing. It was weird. He did it like five or six times."

Lena said to Maggie that she should have come and got her, and she would have gone in to check on him.

"I was just about to," said Maggie. "But then I heard a loud 'Shhh'. At least that's what it sounded like. And after that it got real quiet. I guess I fell asleep."

The very next night, shortly after Wayne had decided he had had enough television and climbed into bed alongside Lena, and barely enough time for the darkness to chase out the light, Aaron came into their room complaining of hearing voices outside his room.

According to Lena, Wayne put him back to bed, and convinced him along the way that there was nobody else in the house; that there were no monsters or bad men under his bed or in his closet; and although Aaron insisted the voices were in the hallway, Wayne promised he'd go have a look outside, which he did, going out on the deck in his bare feet and pajamas and standing outside Aaron's window so he could see him. Before coming back to bed, he went back into Aaron's room to tuck him in and make sure Aaron was convinced.

This same event happened two or three more times over the next week. Each time Wayne performed the same ritual, and each time Aaron was satisfied and went off to sleep without further disruption.

Then came the monster in the closet incident. According to Lena, up until then and for a period of almost two weeks, there had been little to no activity.

"There were a couple of nights in a row," she said, "during which both Wayne and I heard children's voices. They were really low, as if they knew we were sleeping—or at least trying to, and there was some giggling. But we'd just ask them nicely to go away and leave us alone, and then we'd hear the sound of their little feet go pitter-pattering away. Other than that, there was nothing else to speak of.

"But then Emma gave us a pretty big scare. It was definitely in June, and just before school was letting out for the summer. I had put Emma to bed, read her a story, and made sure as I pulled the door partially closed as I left that her nightlight was on. She won't fall asleep unless the light is on and the door a touch open. Both Maggie and Aaron were in their rooms, too, watching television, or whatever they do. It was too early for bed for them; I'd say 7:30, maybe 8:00 at the latest.

"I had been in the family room maybe twenty minutes. The TV was on, but I was reading my book and enjoying a cold drink. Suddenly, Emma lets out a scream the likes of which I have never in my life heard, and especially from her. I immediately bolted up out of the recliner and ran down the hallway. Maggie was coming out of her room at the same time, and Aaron was standing to the other side of the door of his room, the door open just enough for him to peek out.

"I pushed open the door to Emma's room. She was sitting up in bed, her blankets and sheets on the floor—completely off the bed as if someone had pulled them off, and her eyes wide open. She seemed to be frozen. It took a few minutes of me holding and rocking her and telling her everything was alright before she seemed to come out of it.

"When she did, she started to cry. By this time, Maggie had come into the room, and Aaron was standing in the hall and looking through the door. When Emma was finally ready to talk, she said there was a monster in the room and it tried to take her. Of course, I assured her it was only a nightmare, a bad dream, and that there were no real monsters. But Emma was insistent, saying again that the monster grabbed up the blanket and sheet and threw them to the floor. It then reached for her, and that's when she screamed.

"Maggie came over by the bed with me, gathering up the blanket and sheet from the floor on the way, and setting them back in place. She too said things to make Emma feel better. And that's when Emma said the monster ran into the closet. The closet door was slightly open. I'd like to say that I know it was closed when I first put her to bed, but the truth is I had no idea.

"But then Maggie said to Emma that there was nothing in the closet, and went over to show her. 'See,' she said as she pulled open the door. I think all three of us screamed at the same time. As the door came open, we all saw a definite shape, as if outlined by some faint aura against the dark. It was as tall as Maggie, slender and thin limbed, had what I'd describe as a pear-shaped head—but narrow, and a dull or pale glint to white eyes like little circles. It looked right at me—at least I thought it did, and then seemed to dematerialize, just fade. It all happened so quickly. One instant it was there, and the next it wasn't.

"Emma was crying by this time, while Maggie and I just froze in place, looking first into the dark of the closet and then at each other. Aaron, too was crying—although he didn't know why—and refused to come into the room.

"Needless to say, I took Emma out of the room and put her to bed in my room. It also took Maggie and me some time to calm down Aaron. By the time we had managed to convince him that Maggie and I had simply let our imaginations get away with us, that what we saw was just Emma's clothes hanging there, we had managed to also convince ourselves. We chalked it up to the other incidents, and left it at that."

By this time, Lena and I had completed four sessions of hypnosis. After each of these sessions, we would have a follow-up session in which I would debrief her. These debriefing sessions were also recorded, and routinely included the two of us listening to the audio recorded while Lena was under hypnosis.

With regard to this last session, she was surprised at her own description of the presence in the closet. While she and Maggie both agreed they saw something that night, despite the fact that they rationalized otherwise, neither recalled any specific details. And while the detail under hypnosis was nothing to write home about, it was significant as compared to no detail at all.

The particular conversation that was to follow included all the questions I would have expected. Nevertheless, I shied away from any type of speculation, and reminded her that's why we were doing this. Our intent was first to surface anything that might be subconsciously suppressed, and then when the time came, to see what we could make of it. We were, however, I assured her, not yet at that point.

THE SUMMER OF 2009

It was actually on July 4th that the next significant paranormal event there within the house took place. According to Lena, the family had gone together to a fireworks display down in Roosevelt. By the time they arrived back to the house in Lapoint, both Emma and Aaron had fallen asleep in the car. She and Wayne let Emma sleep, with dad carrying her into the house and putting her to bed, but they woke Aaron. He was getting too big to carry.

Despite the late hour, it was a fight to get Aaron to go into bed. The short nap had recharged his batteries. Both she and Wayne compromised, and while even Maggie had called it a night, they said he could have the television on in his room. At the worst, she thought, she'd go in later and turn it off. But she too fell asleep, as did Wayne.

It was 3:42 in the morning, she recalled, when she suddenly had the feeling there was someone there in the room with her—besides Wayne. She opened her eyes to find Aaron standing beside her bed and looking down at her. His face was expressionless.

She asked him if he was feeling well, and he said there was a little man in his room. Had they not been through so much already, she would have attributed it to his imagination and the television. She first thought of waking Wayne, but when she glanced over at him, he was once again sleeping flat on his back and appeared as stiff as a board. His breathing, too, was shallow, but steady. He looked peaceful, but completely out of it.

She took Aaron by the hand and together they went back into his room. Besides Tonto, who barely bothered to look up when they entered, there was nothing there. She even checked the closet, half-expecting what she saw the last time. She found only the usual. Regardless, she thought for sure Aaron was going to want to come back and get into bed with them. He surprised her though by saying he was okay.

Sitting on the edge of the bed with him for a few minutes, she asked him what he thought he saw. He pointed to his three-drawer dresser and said, 'A little man, no higher than that.' He went on to say it was an Indian, and older than a boy but younger than a man. He was naked with only a knot of black hair atop his head which looked like a short pony tail. His teeth were small and pointed, and had space between them. He also said that the little man had no private parts.

When Lena asked him how he was able to see so much in the dark, Aaron told her it wasn't dark. It was light, just not like in the day time.

She then asked him if the television was on, but he said no, that he had turned it off before he went to sleep.

When she asked him where the little Indian came from, he said the wall, pointing over towards the one with the window to the side of the house, not the one to the back.

"But it wasn't like that, not like it is now," he said.

Asking him to explain, he said it was like the wall wasn't there, but it wasn't outside either. "It was like there was a hole there," he said. "Like a worm hole in space, or like a void. But not like in the movies or on TV. There were no stars or zooming lights. It was all gold-like, like when the fire starts to go out in the fireplace. And the little Indian man climbed through and came into the room."

She asked him what the little man did when he came into the room.

Aaron shrugged. "Nothing," he said. "He just stood there. But when Tonto got up, he showed his teeth, then turned around and hopped back through the opening. That's when the wall turned back into the wall, and I came and got you."

When she discussed it with Wayne the next morning, he seemed a bit skeptical, attributing the whole thing to Aaron's imagination, the television, and his preoccupation with UFOs and stuff. He

In the Shadow of the Ridge

reminded her, too, that Aaron recently saw the movie with the Indian action figure that comes alive.

Later, when Aaron came in for cereal, Wayne asked him if there was anything he wanted to talk about. Aaron said no. Wayne then asked him to tell him about the little Indian he saw in his room.

According to Lena, Aaron's face scrunched up a little and he drew his lower lip beneath his upper one. He then said, "It came out of the wall and then went back in. That's all."

So they let it go.

But things didn't end there with Aaron. He was soon after to experience a number of encounters with an entity he described as a young girl, age thirteen or so.

As we did following all debriefing sessions, Lena and I would meet to continue her narrative, something we intended to do until we were both satisfied all bases had been covered. In this particular session, Lena told me of Aaron's encounters with this girl. I then used the details she provided to guide the session under hypnosis, again always with the objective to surface anything that may have been suppressed. The difference here, though, was that it was Aaron who saw the girl and not Lena; therefore she would not have had the opportunity to suppress anything related to those encounters.

That said, Lena recalled one particular afternoon in which only she and Emma were in the house. The older kids were off with friends, and Wayne was at work. She states she was seated at the dining room table reading and answering some email on her laptop. Emma was in her room taking a nap, and Tonto was lying there at her feet taking one of his own.

Suddenly, Tonto's head popped up; he looked up at her, and then immediately jumped to his feet. He glanced at her one more time and then took off running in the direction of the kids' rooms.

Lena followed without hesitation, her worry being something was wrong with Emma. Dogs can sense those kind of things, she said.

But when she again had Tonto in her sight, he was pawing and sniffing at the bottom of the door leading into Aaron's room. She came up behind him, saying his name and asking what was the matter. Tonto was by this time whining excitedly and looking back and forth between her and the door. She stopped by the door and listened, but didn't hear anything. Cautiously, she grasped the door knob and began to slowly push the door open. Although Tonto was not a big dog, he was big and strong enough to push past her and into the room. He scooted around the bed and towards the window to the side of the house. Suddenly, he pulled up and leaped involuntarily backwards as if encountering something he didn't expect. He then set himself in a crouch and was growling at the thin air in front of him. He barked twice and as menacingly as Lena could recall. Then just like that his whole demeanor relaxed and he turned and trotted back the short distance to where Lena was standing, sitting at her feet and looking up at her triumphantly, eyes bright and tail wagging. She remembered patting his head and telling him 'good boy'.

"I was certain," she was to say afterwards, "that there was something there, something that Tonto could see, but I couldn't."

Following that incident, she recalled under hypnosis, a number of times where she'd be down by the kids' rooms for whatever reason—putting away or looking for laundry, vacuuming, or just checking in on the kids—and hear Aaron talking. She assumed he was simply playing with his action figures. She never stood around long enough to actually listen to what he was saying.

That was not the case a sunny afternoon late in July. Only she and Aaron were at home, Maggie having taken Emma on a play date. Lena was working out in the flower beds at the front of the house, pulling weeds and raking the soil. Tonto was out there with her, lying in the shade.

In the Shadow of the Ridge

Just as was so with the dining room, his head suddenly popped up with both ears pricked up and twitching. He then scrambled up to his feet and tore full speed around to the north side of the house. Her first thought was he had detected a porcupine. For some reason, he had a thing for porcupines. He'd go nuts whenever he caught the scent or sight of one. Although they tended to stay up in the rocks, every now and then one would come down close to the house. Wayne said it was for the water. He also said that Tonto's luck was running out, that eventually he'd actually catch one, and he'd be sorry after that.

He was out of sight only a matter of seconds, before Lena heard his barking and whining. It was both excited and intense, and she was concerned that maybe he had cornered something. She got up out of the dirt and went around to the side of the house where she saw Tonto raised up on his back legs and his front paws working hard to get through the screened window into Aaron's room. As the screen started to shred, he was doing all he could to get through the window, leaping and jabbing his snout into the ever-widening opening.

More concerned with the damage he was doing, Lena ran over, hooked his collar, and pressed him firmly from the window and to the ground. With all four paws back on the ground, he spun, and came right back up again at her side. She stated it was then that she saw Aaron. He was totally oblivious to both her and Tonto, despite all the noise and commotion. Somewhat mesmerized herself, she watched as he crossed-legged and sitting on his bed seemed to be deeply involved in conversation with someone that wasn't there. Try as she might, she couldn't get his attention. At first she contemplated trying to go in through the window herself, but instead ran around to the front of the house, flew in through the front door, and got to his room as fast as she could, Tonto at her heels.

As she pushed the door open, Tonto squirmed past her, almost taking her off her feet. Growling and snarling, he leaped onto the bed in front of Aaron, who to this point remained oblivious. The dog's momentum, however, carried him in one bound off the surface of the bed and to the floor on the other side. At this point, Aaron came out of whatever trance he was in and calmly said, "Hi, Mom."

When we spoke about this incident during the debriefing, Lena said that for the longest while Aaron professed to have no memory of it, and that whenever she brought it up, he'd become frustrated with her.

"We were coming back from one of his baseball games," she said. "It was towards the end of the summer before we sold the house. He had just turned thirteen. It was just the two of us, so we decided to stop for ice cream. I noticed that while we were inside the store he was looking pretty intently over at a girl who was seated at one of the tables with what I presume was her family. He was getting to that age, so that he'd be attracted to a cute girl his age wasn't any surprise. I remember getting a bit of a smile out of it.

"Well, when we got back into the car, he was really quiet for a minute or so. As we got close to where we turn off 121 to go home, he said to me, 'Mom, do you remember that time when I was little and you came into the room because you thought I was talking to someone?'

"Of course, I remembered. But I down played it so that he'd keep going. He then told me that the girl in Friendly's looked just like her—the same age and with the same long brown hair and dark eyes. The only difference, he said, was that whenever he saw her, she was always wearing pajama top and bottoms. He said the pajamas had burn holes down the back, on one of her shoulders, and down the leg. He said the holes appeared charred at the edges. And she was wet, as if someone had tried to douse the flames. 'I

In the Shadow of the Ridge

always knew when she was there,' he said, 'because there was always a smoky smell. If I tried not to pay attention to her, she'd peg me with Legos until I looked over at her.'

"I asked him what would happen then. He said they'd talk, but he didn't remember much about it, only that she wanted to know where her parents were and her brother and sister. He said she missed them very much, and that they had gotten lost, or it was she who did.

"I asked him if he saw her a lot. He said it was only a few times. Apparently, she didn't like Tonto and all his barking. So once Tonto started sleeping in his room at nights, she stopped coming around. When I asked him what she wanted, he said only that he was the only one that could see her—besides the dog, and he thought she needed his help. 'But I don't think I could have helped her,' he said. 'She was already dead.'

"Obviously, that freaked me out a little. But given what we had all already gone through, and the house was sold, I just let it go. He still brings it up every now and then, but it's more like an inside joke when he does, and he doesn't seem to be afraid."

THE UNEXPLAINED DISABILITY

The holidays came around, and my sessions with Lena took a short hiatus. During that time, and consistent with what we had done since we were married, Jessica and I had continued to see specialists. She was concerned that her biological clock was ticking and that if she didn't conceive soon that she never would.

"You know the statistics as well as I do," she said, by way of motivation—not hers, but mine. "The odds of complications as the woman ages go up significantly. You men get all the breaks."

Although I never admitted it to her, and even hesitate to say as much now, I had pretty much given up the idea of having children. If it wasn't to be, then it wasn't to be.

But the truth was, despite all the visits to previous doctors and specialists, not a single test had detected anything that ruled out the physical possibility. The only facts we had were that my sperm count was normal, as was my ability to inseminate. And while more than one of these learned professionals had agreed there was something to the previous diagnosis concerning the ovulation process, there was nothing definite precluding the possibility. The consistent response was patience and frequent and routine intimacy.

Right after Christmas, Jessica and I decided on impulse to take a trip out to Las Vegas. We caught a flight out of Vernal early that Wednesday and were casino hopping well before the ball dropped. After all the horn blowing, confetti flying, and cork popping, we went back to our hotel room and ushered in the New Year in our own fashion.

I had no reason at the time to believe we were successful, but we both came home happy and with a whole bunch less stress.

The sessions with Lena started up again the second to last week of January. We had reached the point in her narrative at which she herself had been personally targeted by the entity or entities present at their home.

As was our routine, I permitted Lena to take the initiative in a non-hypnosis induced session in which she would tell me whatever came to mind about a particular incident, after which I would use the details provided to conduct the session under hypnosis.

She recalled it was the third week in August, and school had just started. She remembered waking up from a deep sleep, thinking that she had overslept and the kids would be late. The room, however, was still very dark, with no hint of early morning light seeping through any of the blinds. She tried to turn her head to look at the clock, and found she couldn't do so. Her first thought was that there was something terribly wrong, that she might have had a stroke, or something similar. She calmed herself and did an immediate mental check. She didn't feel any pain, and although she found that none of her limbs were responding to her, she could very much feel the sheets as the lay upon her, the soft indent to the pillow to the back of her head, and that if she really focused hard enough on it, that she could move her finger and toes, and even roll her feet from side to side.

Feeling the panic rising up in her, she tried to wake Wayne, doing the only thing which she could do, which was to call his name. But regardless of how frustrated she grew or the effort she made, her voice sounded thin and without urgency. And although she had only her peripheral vision and the merest ability to turn her head, she could see that he had once again adopted that upon-his-back rigid posture. She knew he was dead to the world.

Not that she intended to do so, but she drifted back off to sleep. It was Wayne's shaking and nudging which woke her. Having little recall, at least at the moment, of her earlier situation, she thought to get up, but found she couldn't. Her body was not responding to her.

Wayne, as would be expected, was very concerned, and he too immediately jumped to the conclusion that she had suffered a stroke. He called the police and within ten minutes or so, there was an ambulance outside the house.

The EMTs came in, and with all the kids in Maggie's room, and Wayne going back and forth assuring them Lena was going to be okay, Lena was subjected to the usual protocols. According to what she was told, all of her vital signs were normal and she was in no immediate distress. Nevertheless, it was clearly determined that she was suffering from some sort of paralysis not-paralysis, or at the very least some extreme weakness. Either way, she was going to the hospital. She was taken to the Medical Center in Vernal.

Upon arrival, she was brought into the emergency room where she was transferred to a bed behind one of the many curtains which they wheeled her past. Outside of any obvious concern for her condition, she was otherwise in no discomfort.

She was treated by an emergency room doctor who seemed utterly perplexed by her symptoms. Speaking to both Wayne and Lena—Maggie was left at home to care for Aaron and Emma, and Wayne's mother was on the way there, she first confirmed what the EMTs had said as for the normalcy of her blood pressure, heart rate, body temperature, eye activity, and everything else that she could determine without more formal testing. She then recommended a CAT scan and an MRI, and made arrangement for Lena to be brought up to a room.

The CAT scan, according to Lena, took place later on that morning, and then the MRI the day following. Neither one showed anything of concern. Yet without an explanation that made sense, the doctor arranged to extend her stay with the expectation that the condition could very possibly resolve itself. In the interim, more blood samples were taken to test for potential bacterial or viral infection.

Lena explained that these, too, came back negative.

In the Shadow of the Ridge

By this time, she had been in the hospital almost a full week. She missed her children, despite their daily visits, and wanted to go home.

When I asked her to tell me about what she was feeling and thinking while lying there, she told me only that she couldn't help but think either the doctors were missing something, or there was something going on that was beyond them.

"However, when I slept at night, I found myself having these dreams," she said. "But they weren't normal. I was dreaming things that had no sense to them, as if they didn't belong to me. Obviously in the dreams, I was some place, but they weren't places that were familiar. I can only describe as if I was dreaming someone else's dreams.

"And that's not all of it. They just didn't seem like dreams. I don't think I can explain it."

That's when I told her not to worry about it, that we'd explore the subject at greater length under hypnosis. I then changed the topic to her release from the hospital.

"It was just like the doctor had said. I woke up that second to last night there, and though my muscles all felt kind of spongy, I was able to move. I was so happy and relieved, I tried to get up out of bed, but when I put my feet on the floor to stand up, my legs went all rubbery, and it was all I could do not to spill all over the floor. The funny thing is I was looking forward to using the toilet; I had a catheter plugged into me.

"I gave a thought to calling for the nurse, but decided it'd wait for morning. I laid back in bed and did some little exercises to wake my limbs back up, just lifting each leg one at a time and flexing my arms, things like that. I'm not sure what time it was. There was no clock. But I fell back asleep.

"That morning when the nurse came in, I was already sitting up and greeted her with a wave and a smile. The doctor came in a while later when I was having breakfast—the first meal which hadn't been spoon fed to me, literally, in eight days. Despite my objection, she and Wayne convinced me to stay one more day to do some physical therapy—which I did. I was home before noon the day following."

Under hypnosis, Lena provided a significantly different perspective on her ailment. All the details of which were relative to her sleeping hours. Throughout, her tone was matter-of-fact. She referred routinely to being possessed by a presence which professed the intent to take over her 'animal'.

When asked to expound on what she meant by *possessed*, she insisted that there was a substantial presence that was trying to push into her. She said she was fully aware of being her, but as if at a distance to herself. She described struggling, as if resisting some force which was trying to push or expel her from her own body, and at the same time cramming itself into whatever space the process had managed to free up. She insisted that presence was fully within her, but not in control.

"It was as if," she said, "it had no idea what to do once it was inside of me. But I could feel it, not sharing my thoughts, but its own thoughts existing alongside my own, like a whispering voice or one without substance.

"During the day when I was fully awake, I guess all the stimulus was overwhelming it: the things I was seeing, the things I was hearing, and perhaps the interaction with the nurses coming and going; it was all too much for it. I knew it was still there, but I imagined it curled up in a fetal position somewhere dark and removed.

"But at night, when it was quiet and there was hardly anyone around, it would again become aggressive, referring constantly to 'my animal' or 'this animal'. It was then that I'd most feel the pushing or pulling, whatever, and that distance from myself increasing.

"I don't think it was strong enough or perhaps confident enough, because each time I would catch myself drifting mentally, sort of losing contact with myself, I would push back; and it would relent. This would go on for I don't know how long, but I think the struggle, the effort, made it just as weak as it did me.

"All I know is I would eventually fall asleep and then slip into these dreams, mostly of a place that wasn't any place I know, or even recognized. And although any detail would have left me by the time I awoke, I was always left with the memory of something completely alien to any place that I have ever been or ever seen. A place of waiting, I'd call it.

"What I do remember, however, is a dark figure there in the room. Before I saw him, I smelled him, or at least there was a smell, an odor. I say odor because it wasn't pleasant. It was rank and humid. When I was a girl, we had a family dog named Heidi, like the girl in the movie. We had that dog for almost 20 years, and that's no exaggeration. When she had gotten real old, and just before we found her dead out on the back porch, I remember her hair had gotten oily and she had this really pungent odor, worse than when dogs are wet. I stopped petting her because of that. The smell would get on your hands. It was nasty. Anyway, that's the kind of odor that was in the room. But I'm not saying it was exactly that.

"Whatever this figure was, it wasn't a nurse, or doctor, or attendant of any kind. I am certain that I was asleep. And if not fully asleep, then in that stage between, when you're not sure if you're awake or dreaming. I can still see it, standing there by the side of my bed and looking down at me. All I know is that it reached towards me, and the next thing I know I'm sitting upright in the bed, and my right arm pushing out against an arm and presence that wasn't there.

"That's when I realized I was moving. I remember the effort it took to fold back the bed sheet and blanket and swing my feet to the floor. I tried to get up, to stand up, but my legs felt like rubber.

Despite the fact that I really wanted to use the bathroom, I gave up and laid back in the bed. I remember the pressure in my bladder easing as it emptied through the catheter. I know I lie there for a while taking pleasure in just moving my arms and legs. After that, I must have dozed back off. And I remember as I did being aware that I was again myself, and that whatever it was that was trying to possess me, to possess my animal, was no longer present. It was gone."

Back at home, Lena took it easy and worked at getting back her strength. Two times a week she had appointments with a physical therapist in Roosevelt. Other than that, she pretty much remained in the house, with Wayne running most of the errands. Emma was in pre-school most of the mornings, and Lena's mother-in-law would come in the afternoons, and then remain to prepare supper. She also would routinely burn shavings of cedar as incense to keep dark spirits from the home. Lena didn't mind. She liked the aroma, and it reminded her of her own grandmother. This particular routine continued for the better part of a month, after which she finally convinced Wayne's mother that she was pretty much back to normal.

During that particular period of time, Lena was certain there was no paranormal activity of any sort going on, though she does remember Tonto making a bit of a commotion one night, which woke her. She said she had some distant thoughts of there being something outside her window, and she again thought werewolf. But then Tonto settled down. She did remember thinking it odd, however, that he was not at the time in Aaron's room, which was where he always slept.

The last incident, she remembers, then, and this before the portal incident, took place in early November. It had started to snow while the kids were in school, so that by the time they got home, there was a couple of inches on the ground. By the time she and the kids had finished dinner, those couple of inches had grown to five. She asked Maggie to help her shovel some of the driveway so that Wayne would have a fairly clean spot to park in. He was working late that night, and by the way the snow was still falling, she thought a couple more inches, at least, were possible.

When they went out through the garage with shovels in hand, the skies had already darkened. There were, however, spot lights to light up the driveway. She and Maggie had been out there for about a half hour and making petty good progress, when at the same time they both heard what they thought to be a chorus of voices sweep down from the hills at the back of the house, roll over their heads, and echo again off the rise to the south where the neighbor's property sits. Though the enunciation was somewhat muted, and sounds can be confused by so much rock and stone, Lena said they were both convinced that what they heard was, "Lena's back, Lena's back."

This went on for what seemed like eternity, she said, but was probably only seconds. Maggie got really scared, and said she wanted to go back in the house. With no doubt whatsoever that they heard what they heard, she and Maggie left the shovels where they stood and with her arms wrapped around her daughter, they hurried back in to the garage, Lena hitting the pad to close the door behind them, and the two of them making straight for the door into the house. No sooner did the garage door touch the floor, they both heard a loud groan rumble down from the ridge. So intense it was, it rattled the house so that Aaron had jumped up from his position on the floor in front of the television in the family room, and Emma had started to cry.

Lena said she immediately lit the cedar, and she and the kids sat huddled on the couch until Wayne came home.

THE PORTAL

The portal incident was revealed by Lena in what was to be one of our last sessions. We met only twice after that, one of which was the hypnosis session and the other the debriefing. Following the debriefing session, Lena had stopped by the office unannounced. She had brought Emma with her. She apologized for coming by without a formal appointment, but, she said, she was nearby running errands, and on the way back home Emma asked if Lena would bring her to the office. She said she tried explaining to Emma about appointments, but she nonetheless became very insistent. Given all that we had done up to that point, meaning Lena and I and the sessions, and how Emma fit into the picture—she was, after all, Lena's impetus for coming to me in the first place; well, as she said at the time, "Here we are."

As for the portal incident, Lena recalled she had agreed to take Maggie up to the Lapoint reservoir to take photos for an art class project. Maggie had been bugging Lena to do so for a couple of weeks, and Lena, for some reason kept putting it off. Finally, Maggie, frustrated by the delay, came into the kitchen shortly after dinner had been finished and declared that she was going to walk out there by herself. She had on her coat, gloves, and ski-cap with her long brown hair spilling out from beneath. Her camera was in hand.

Lena told her she didn't think it was a good time. It was already getting late, and with the coyotes being nocturnal, among other things, she preferred that Maggie wait, and she'd take her after she came home from school that next day.

Maggie, however, professed that it would be too late, that the photos were needed for tomorrow's class.

Lena's first impulse was to admonish her for waiting to the last minute, but readily admitted that wasn't the case, that she herself

In the Shadow of the Ridge 105

was the responsible party. Nevertheless, she saw fit to once again point out the approaching darkness. She offered to take her early in the morning before school started.

The expression on Maggie's face was one of immediate disapproval.

Lena conceded. She asked Maggie to help her with Emma. Wayne had taken Aaron to one of those father-son things they did together.

The reservoir—one of a handful in that area—was a man-made water-filled depression about a mile or so north northwest of the house and nestled within the ridge and just this side of the Ouray Canal. At the time of our sessions, due to the lack of rain and melted snow runoff, the water levels were extremely low, and there were local officials warning it soon may run dry. However, Lena remembered the water level looking that night as it always did.

She recalled, too, strapping Emma into the car seat in the back of her Jeep Cherokee, while Maggie hopped up front. She then got in, started the engine, and backed away from the garage at an angle which allowed for her to go down the driveway nose first. She then made the right onto the unpaved stretch of Mountain Road and headed north towards the reservoir. There was absolutely nothing along the way, she said, that had anything to do with civilization or modern convenience: no street lights, no road signs, and not a single house.

About a half mile or so up, she found the turnoff she was looking for, and made the right onto another dirt road—it had no official name—which was less traveled and more of a challenge. About another half mile, and she would come to a fork. Stay to the right, and she'd be at the reservoir. Got to the left, and she'd be heading west towards the canal. She had never gone that far herself; that particular stretch of road was very rough.

She described the reservoir as little more than an isolated lake scooped out of the barren rock and dirt, its banks hard and stone-colored, and with only the occasional spot of scrub brush here and there. To the west, she said, was nothing but pale hills and clustered formations of pale colored rock, while to the east and north, the rock of the ridge dropped from high up at a precipitous angle down to the water's edge. She then made the point that just a short distance further up and to the east were the actual peaks or spine of the ridge, which ran from there in a straight line practically to their back door. Altogether, she thought it a desolate and alien place. She did admit, however, that she and Wayne had gone out that way a few times when the moon was full, or after a snowfall, and if the mood was right, it could be quite romantic.

Continuing her narrative, she said they came to the fork she was looking for, and rolled the vehicle slowly along the path, coming to a stop among the thin band of trees which were to each side. Maggie immediately popped out of the Cherokee and went ahead on her own. By the time Lena had managed freeing Emma from the car seat, Maggie already had descended the hundred or so yards down to the reservoir edge and was snapping away. The sky, Lena recalled, had a particularly peaceful glow to it, the lowering sun tracing the crests of the hills to the west with a pale orange glow, while up overhead was darkening to a bluish-gray. She remembered thinking that it was a beautiful setting for Maggie's photos.

As for anything out of the normal happening when they were out there, Lena mentioned only some behavior involving Emma. While Maggie, as teen girls do, was doing her best imitation of independence, making sure to go off in whatever direction was opposite that of Lena and Emma, Lena said she was occupied keeping track of Emma, who was bopping about without a care in the world.

"I found that a little strange," she mused. "Usually when we are out and about, Emma is a clinger. And even if she wants to go up to something, she'll grab my hand and try to drag me along. But not that night. It was all I could do to keep her within reach and keep an eye on Maggie.

"I remember taking a glance over to where Maggie was taking photos, making sure she wasn't getting to close to the water's edge. When I looked back to Emma, she was a good distance from me, giggling and running about in circles as if she was chasing something. When I asked her what she was doing, she said she was trying to catch the light balloons."

Lena went on to add that neither she nor Maggie saw anything of the sort, and then acknowledged having heard from the time she herself was a little girl similar stories of balls and spheres of light moving around the desert at night. She said her grandmother told her they were the spirits of the Holy people. However, she said she also read somewhere that scientists referred to them as anomalies of some sort. It had something to do with the rock.

According to Lena, they were out there for about an hour, after which Maggie made the declaration that she had accomplished all she was going to accomplish, and she was ready to go back home. Lena chased down and corralled Emma, and with a mother's scoop, had her in arms, and together the three of them made their way back to the vehicle.

Shortly thereafter, Lena said, everything went strange.

She strapped in Emma, and with Maggie alongside her, put the car in drive and went forward to circle around and head back out in the direction from which they had come. No sooner had she cleared the line of trees going the other direction, she recalled a sudden pressure build in her ears similar to that of when in an airplane and it ascends to that height. Maggie felt it too, and said as much. Oddly enough though, Emma had already nodded out. Her eyes were closed and her head pushed back in the car seat. Her face was peaceful.

The following narrative is taken from the actual transcript of the session audio:

"The discomfort quickly passed," said Lena. "But I couldn't help feeling that something wasn't right. I remember saying to Maggie I'll be glad when we pull into the driveway. I had more than half expected her to tell me to stop being silly, but instead she said 'me, too'.

"I clearly remember making the turn onto the road which leads back to Mountain Road. But then about halfway back there's this stretch that curves around and into these high hills to the west and the base of the ridge to the east, where the rock is really high up too. It's like one s-curve running into another. It's also a dead zone where you can't get a cell phone signal.

"And that's when everything went crazy. I suddenly became extremely disoriented, with this queasy feeling in my stomach. I tried to keep it together, but I had this sudden realization that I had no idea where I was. Way back in my head, there was this flicker of recognition of things; but it was as if there was something there, too, which wouldn't let my brain make any connections. Every time I caught a glimpse of something I thought I recognized, it dissolved almost immediately in a puddle of confusion. There was absolutely no continuity to any of my thoughts. It was as if someone was flicking the lights on and off, and each time that fraction of a second it was light again, I was seeing something completely different.

"All I know is I kept driving, fighting a surge of panic, and convinced, or at least trying to convince myself, that at any moment everything would be alright. Like I said, there was this little voice somewhere behind all of the confusion telling me that I had to be where I thought I was.

"It then came to me that I should look over at Maggie. She was sitting there as still as a mannequin, her mouth hanging open and her stare distant. I remember thinking I should reach over and shake her. And just then I lost control of the car, or control was taken from me. It was nothing violent, but we went off the road, off the dirt path, and sliding almost sideways. I felt the passenger side go up as we hit the upward slope of the rock, and I felt for sure we were going to roll over. But then just as suddenly, the nose hit a depression, and the back of the vehicle started to spin counter-clockwise. I watched in a way that was way too detached as the front end turned toward this huge boulder, and I thought for sure we were going to hit it. Instead, the car stopped turning and just slid parallel up a ways a little more, and then came to a stop.

"The next thing I know I'm aware of Emma crying. It was then that the whole spinning car came back to me, and in near panic I looked into the back seat certain that she had been thrown about. But she was still safely strapped in and didn't appear to be hurt or shaken in any way. Maggie, too, was okay, at least from what I could see, but completely out of it. It took a couple of tries, but I was able to both calm down Emma, who I thought cranky more than anything else, and bring Maggie around. She was obviously disoriented, and kept asking where we were.

"I told her we had a bit of an accident with the car, but that we were all okay, and that I'd get us home. The car, thankfully, was still running, and I was able to get it back onto the road with no trouble. We were in the driveway five minutes later."

The funny part, she then said, was that by the clock in the house—which was always in time with her cellphone, they had been gone for somewhat more than an hour. The time on her cellphone, however, which was from what she could tell was working fine, had somehow lost about 8 or 9 minutes.

She chalked it up to some anomaly of the mountains and rock, and simply reset it.

The session in which we addressed this incident under hypnosis did not yield significantly different details up and until the moment Lena drives along that particular point in the road in which she became disoriented. From that moment until she becomes aware of Emma's crying there is notable deviation.

According to Lena, as you come to that part of the road where it first curves, the rocks are tight on both sides and rise up high and pretty much at a 90° angle. To make things worse, at that particular time of night, the sudden absence of light and the density to the darkness was very disconcerting. What she remembers quite vividly, though, under hypnosis was being able to see clearly all around her, as if she was peering through some sort of night vision device—the kind which she had only heard about or seen on television, but herself had never used or experienced. She called it light not-light. She described it as varying shades and intensities of the same color spectrum, but even under hypnosis could not provide for the color. She vacillated between amber and sepia, but wouldn't state with certainty, regardless of how much I coached her, whether it was more one than the other, or if either at all. She maintained, however, that all about her was a single color, with the only variation being the shade or intensity distinguishing depth and distance. Other than that, she recalled only stone and rock and the dirt road.

At this point in our session, she then grew quiet and still and required from me some degree of coaxing before she went on. I first attempted to get her to provide me with more detail about her surroundings. But this focus proved fruitless. She remained silent and her eyes staring. She, however, did not exhibit any sign of distress. Using details from the previous session, I then suggested her daughters, any sounds she might be hearing, or anything visually curious. Again, she made no verbal response. Finally, I asked her to feel the steering wheel in her hand. Her posture became observably more rigid, and she again began to recount the incident.

She spoke first of an overwhelming sense of panic accompanying the irrational realization that she had no idea where she was. She remembers holding on to the wheel with all the grip she could muster, believing it her only tether to reality. Try as she might to focus her eyes out beyond the windshield, she was distracted by a keen awareness of sensory deprivation.

She reported then feeling intense anxiety, followed by an overwhelming and sudden sense of depression. Then it seemed, she started hallucinating. "The rock and stone are rushing towards us," she said, followed by, "They're going to hit us, crash through the windshield."

So intense was this moment of recall that she shut her eyes and flinched while sitting there in my office. Then came a pause, during which time she remained unmoving, as if expecting to be hit. The moment passed, after which she again opened her eyes, her posture still defensive, and continued. "I don't feel the car moving, but everything around us says it is. My hands—at least I see as much—are on the steering wheel still, my foot upon the pedal, but there is no signal to my brain telling me that I'm touching either. I'm completely detached from any physical sensation, as if everything that was the conscious aware me was now someplace else, removed at a distance, but close enough for me to know it's me that I'm distant from." She then said she was one-hundred percent certain that they were going to crash head-on into the rock, and simply resigned herself to the inevitable.

Lena then recalled that, as the moment hung, she looked over at Maggie and didn't see her. She looked away, fighting off a feeling of indifference, and then looked back again. Maggie was there. But she recognized nothing about her that was Maggie. "It was Maggie physically," she said, "but no more so than a mannequin would be." She looked away and back one more time, and again she wasn't there. Instead, she said, that side of the car seemed to have dematerialized. She saw only rock and dirt, and that too seemed to

112 **In the Shadow of the Ridge**

be moving towards and away from her at the same time. Then, as if random images were being flashed in her head, or perhaps pulled from it, she caught a glimpse of Emma. This image was then followed by a thought she found at the time both odd and comforting. It was as if a voice was telling her there was no reason to be concerned for Emma. Nodding and her tone matter-of-fact, Lena repeated, "Emma's in no danger."

At this point in the session, Lena again grew quiet, and to be truthful, non-responsive to any of my attempts to encourage her to go on. I made the decision to end the session, and no sooner did I sit up to bring her out, she again started to speak. I found this to be inconsistent with my own experience, but ultimately was glad that she did. I decided later on to interpret her pause as evidence of an absence of conscious awareness there on that road, and not as being wearied by the session, for example, or something similar.

To follow is the actual transcript of the last few minutes of the session:

"There was a cacophony of noise—but without substance—drifting all around me, as if there were a thousand hissing snakes on the other side of a hill, or thousands of flying insects all buzzing about at the same time in some distant tree top. But beneath it all, there was something recognizable, another sound, like a voice. Not a bunch of them, but just a single voice and in a language which didn't sound like any I've ever heard.

"And then I heard Emma. She was talking in a low voice, but not whispering. I remember thinking how grown-up she sounded, and not just in the way she was talking, but the things she was saying; not a word of which I remember. And that was all shattered by a scream. It was Maggie. I glanced first in her direction, never thinking anything but that she'd be there in the passenger seat, and then suddenly up and over the wheel, when I realized I was driving and the car moving. And that's when I saw the road had curved in the other direction, and we were already off of it. I slammed on the brake and felt the rear wheels start to slide. There was the sound of dirt and pebbles spraying around us, and then the car started to go into a bit of a spin.

"Funny the things you remember at times like that. Right then and there, I heard Wayne telling me that you always turn into a spin—something that happens often around here with all the snow in winter. So I just started turning the wheel furiously to the right, but the jeep just kept sliding passenger side first right towards this huge boulder in front of us. Somehow though, we missed it. The car came to a jolting halt, and then next thing I remember was Emma crying."

The first thing I asked Lena during the debriefing session was if she had talked with Maggie and Emma about the incident. She said she did speak to Maggie later the next day, after Maggie had come home from school, but not to Emma, who she was certain would bring it up on her own in due time, if at all.

As for Maggie, Lena said she did notice something off about her, but at the time was willing to attribute it to her own imagination, given what she herself had experienced the day before. Nevertheless, with Maggie sitting at the dining room table doing her homework, Lena decided to go for it and asked Maggie if she remembered anything odd or different about what happened.

To Lena's surprise, Maggie described similar sensations to the ones that she herself experienced, including the outer-body feeling.

"She described it," said Lena, "as being on a roller-coaster without feeling any of the vibrations, or the car around you, or even the wind in your face. I thought it was interesting because as far as I know, Maggie has only been on one roller-coaster in her life, and not a very big one at that, and at the time she was maybe Aaron's age, maybe 10."

Lena than went on to say that without much coaxing, Maggie said similar things about the odd light and color, convinced that everything appeared as if sand-colored.

"I didn't like it," she told her mother. "There was something freaky about it, and not just the color. It was like I was on Mars or something, with no air to breathe, and I was some kind of Martian who didn't need air anyway."

When Lena told her about looking over and not seeing her, she said Maggie got that expression you get when something suddenly comes to mind, those kind of things that you wouldn't have known you had forgotten unless someone reminded you.

"You weren't there either," she said. "I was all alone sitting in the middle of nowhere, and everything that was around me was as if it was there and not there at the same time, like I could reach out and touch rock that was so far away, but try as I might, I couldn't reach down far enough to grab a handful of the sand I was sitting on.

"I remember, too," she said, "thinking I was sitting next to myself, only really close as to almost being in the same spot, if you know what I mean, so that I was sort of outside myself; and at the same time I was thinking I needed to get back inside of me and that if I didn't, it really wouldn't matter. Then the next thing I'm looking out the windshield and we're going to crash."

As for Emma, according to Lena, she didn't talk about the incident at all, until she brought it up out of nowhere that next spring. As Lena recalled it, a few weeks prior to doing so, she and Emma were outside in the front yard. It was later in the day, before Maggie and Aaron would get home from school, but after Emma's pre-school; she was already five by then, but Lena and Wayne had made the decision at the beginning of the school-year not to enroll her in kindergarten. Her late birthday would have made her one of the youngest in her class, and they didn't want that, particularly later on in high school where a year can make a big difference, for example in sports or just the level of maturity.

In the Shadow of the Ridge   115

Regardless, Lena was working in the flower beds, pulling weeds and raking the soil, when she just happened to look to see what Emma was up to. She was sitting on the steps to the front door playing with one of Aaron's action figures.

"It was the way the sun caught her eyes," said Lena. "I don't know why I had never noticed it before. But all of my kids have dark brown eyes, even Emma. But the way that the sun hit them, they definitely looked green, and as they moved, I saw they were flecked with intensely bright glints of honey that seemed to dart here and there like fish in a pond breaking the surface of the water for but an instant, and then disappearing again."

It was about two weeks later, according to Lena, that she and Emma were again walking about the yard, when out of nowhere Emma said, "You know, mommy, they put your animal to sleep while they took Maggie and me in the port hole to learn what they needed to learn. They told us they didn't want you to worry."

Lena choked up while telling me this, obviously disconcerted by what she was saying.

"Did you ask her to explain?" I asked.

Lena said she looked down at Emma, and asked, "Why did you say that, honey?"

But Emma only looked at her like she had two heads, and then with a giggle said, "I didn't say anything, mommy."

What could I do but try to assure her?

The day that Lena brought Emma by the office, it was already late and I was just about to leave. In fact, my receptionist had already gone. The door to my office was open, and I remember hearing the outer door to the suite opening. My first thought was that Arnéz, the receptionist, had come back for something. But then I heard a voice saying hello in that questioning way that says 'I'm not sure there's anyone here'. I recognized it as Lena, which initially confused me. I knew that I didn't have anything scheduled—that's why I was going home.

I walked out to greet her, and she immediately apologized for the intrusion. Having seen photos of Emma—what parent these days doesn't have a cell phone full, I recognized her right off. She had her eyes fixed on mine, and though I wasn't seeing any honey-hued sparks, they did appear to be green.

I invited them on in, and once we were in my office, Lena explained the purpose of their visit. She then asked me if it would be okay if she waited outside because Emma had something she wanted to share with me and wanted to do it "in privacy", as it were. I, of course, agreed.

Emma watched her mother leave—she went just outside into the suite, after which she turned and stood there quietly staring at me.

To make things easy for her, I asked, "What would you like to share with me?"

She smiled in a very easy manner, and with an expression that didn't quite go with her nine year-old face, said, "I have a gift for Jessica."

This simple declaration, admittedly, caught me by surprise. "My Jessica?" I asked.

She nodded once. "Your wife."

I guess at the moment, I didn't think anything of it. It made sense that she would know of Jessica. After all, Lena had been to the store a number of times, and Emma herself had received from her mother the turquoise piece.

Coincidentally enough, she then reached into the front pocket of her jeans and came out with a turquoise pendant on a thin silver chain. I immediately made the assumption it was the very piece that Lena had bought.

Without saying anything, she extended the piece to me in her open palm.

"You want my wife to have this?" I asked, lifting it by the chain, so that the pendant itself dangled just above her palm.

She responded by saying, "It's for the baby, actually."

"For the baby?" I repeated. "What baby?"

"Well, for your baby, silly," she answered.

I looked from the pendant up into her face, and was immediately distracted by tiny glints of golden-colored light there behind the green of her eyes.

Catching myself, I started to say "We're not having a baby." But my words fell behind her, as she had already turned and was skipping out the door.

She then stopped but a stride beyond, and turning, she said, "Oh, I almost forgot: Sam's not sad anymore."

That froze me to the spot where I stood, and by the time I had processed what had just taken place, and managed to get to the suite door, Lena and Emma were already in the elevator and on their way down.

I thought a moment about going after them, but then felt an overwhelming need to be home. So I let them go, closed up the office, and hurried to my car.

I remember composing myself up on the porch out back by the garage before going into the house. My plan all the while was to make it a dinner conversation, towards the end when we both would have empty plates in front of us, and enjoying whichever brew we had chosen as the appropriate libation.

When the moment seemed right—a nice segue between her day and mine, I said to her in a way that was probably coyer than I had intended, "I'm not sure if this qualifies yet for the highlight of my day, but I had someone very interesting stop by the office just as I was leaving." I then told Jessica about Lena and Emma, emphasizing that it was the first time I had ever met Emma. I guess I was half-expecting she'd one-up me on this one. But she, too, said that while

Lena had mentioned her children in their conversations, she hadn't met any of them either.

"Well," I said. "This then may come as a bit of a surprise. The reason why they were there was because Emma insisted on it. She had something she wanted to give to me; actually, it was—is— something that she wanted me to give to you."

Jessica didn't say anything, just tipped her head in the way that she does.

I reached into my shirt pocket and pulled out the pendant.

I'm not sure what I expected, but it wasn't the reaction I got.

"Where'd you get that?" she asked, almost with a gasp and definitely somewhat disconcerted.

"I told you. It's from Emma, Lena's daughter."

Jessica reached over and took it from me, and was turning it about in her hand looking at it from every conceivable angle.

"Do you know what this is?" She asked, obviously shaken.

"I assume," I said, "it is the piece that her mother bought from you."

She shook her head slowly from side to side a number of times, and then said, "This is the piece I gave that old Indian for the gold coin."

WHAT IT ALL MEANS

It goes without say that Brad Rogers and I maintained open lines of communication throughout my work with Lena Bishop, with most of that communication taking place via email, and with some phone conversation. However, for the financial compensation I was provided, he and his organization expected and received a formal review of my findings. That document, as a matter of agreement, is both fully confidential and exclusive. The fact, though, that I signed a non-disclosure agreement does not preclude me from summarizing here my personal and professional thoughts on the case, and even going so far as to providing some speculation. I am simply limited by that agreement with regard to certain specifics, primarily refraining from directly or indirectly naming that organization or any of its members or in any way providing information from which any connection to that organization or any of its members may be inferred.

With regard to Lena Bishop, I found no indication that she was to any clinical degree exhibiting a social or psychological pathology of any sort. In other words, she presented as emotionally, psychologically, and cognitively normal. Throughout our sessions, she was at all times personable, intelligent, cogent, emotionally appropriate, open, and rational. At no time did she present as circumventive, deceptive, uncooperative, cryptic, avoiding, manipulative, or fantastic. And while she did present as emotionally invested in her experiences, she was at all times, both when not under hypnosis and when under hypnosis, responsive to inquiry, meaning not stubbornly advocating her own position, and seemingly genuinely interested in resolving her issue, which was an irrational level of anxiety stemming from a belief that her youngest daughter, Emma was, in fact, not her daughter only, but her daughter under the influence of some other entity. While even I felt tempted, at times, to conclude that Lena believed Emma to be *possessed* by some other entity, Lena herself did not ever use that word or even directly imply as much, but instead implied that Emma was either channeling this other entity or that this other entity was animating itself physically through Emma's body. With regard to this issue, I have reserved my response for the conclusion.

As for the incidents or paranormal encounters attributed by Lena to each of the members of her family, I have only Lena's reporting to go on. And these were conditions I accepted from the start. It was made clear to me from day one that neither Lena nor Wayne, and this I know only from Lena, were willing to submit any of their children to an interview process. They were adamant.

According to Lena, as soon as the family moved from the house, which they did early in 2012, there were no further paranormal incidents, and all three of their children seemed to have suppressed any recollection of their encounters and without any negative effect. It was their decision as parents, therefore, to leave things as they were, and to not chance stirring things up again by subjecting the children to a process which by design was intended to do just that. I decided not to pursue the matter.

Later, however, I did ask Lena as to the exact motive of their relocation. She placed the paranormal disturbances and their encounters down low on the list, suggesting instead the feeling of isolation given the location of the house and property, and also some financial stress as a result of certain stipulations attached to the mortgage. As far as I know, the house remains vacant at this time.

What follows is my own speculation on both the case, the primary subject—Lena, and the secondary subjects, specifically the three children, and more so Emma. I stress the fact that this is just my speculation with the knowledge that some people are interested only in the facts, and may choose at this time to read no further. I hope, though, that's not the case; I am rather partial to the end.

To start, I'll begin with Lena and Wayne's encounter of the canine-like animal up on the ridge, for which there are three plausible explanations. The first is that Lena and Wayne encountered a large stray dog. Stray dogs are not an oddity around here. That the animal would appear mangy, scraggy, and emaciated to some degree is reasonable. Not only is the environment challenging, but food sources are scarce, whether with regard to the type of small prey vulnerable to a lone dog on the hunt or the type of foodstuff routinely discarded by humans given the proximity to the Bishop household. Outside of the two immediate neighbors, there were no other houses, stores, or business locations within a mile or more of the location. As for the animal's odd behavior, specifically moving about in a way that seemed to defy logic, it is possible, as Wayne suggested, that the animal was relying on ways around, up into, and through the rock not immediately recognizable to either Wayne or Lena, who admittedly were unfamiliar with the surroundings. The second is that they actually did encounter a Skinwalker, which would account for its abnormal appearance, its seemingly spastic and unnatural gait and movement, and its ability to move in a way which defied natural law, as well as to its sudden and unexplained disappearance, seemingly, into thin air. The third is that Wayne and Lena simply encountered a dog and then embellished the remaining details, or that they didn't encounter a dog of any kind, and that Lena made it all up. That said, there is nothing in my dealings with Lena that would suggest as much. Therefore, if asked to pick one of these three explanations over the others, I'm leaning towards the first.

This brings me then to Lena's werewolf encounters. Given the prominent role of the coyote and wolf, among other animals, in the culture of the Native Americans indigenous to this area, which includes all of the lore associated with the Skinwalker, both with regard to historical applications as well as the more contemporary interpretations—read superstition, it is not unexpected that Lena, or any other individual brought up in that culture, would manifest suppressed anxiety in this way. She herself admitted to being stressed at the time by the move and its potential for stressing her children—specifically leaving behind their friends and starting over at a new school, her own feelings of being disconnected, and the financial considerations associated with home ownership. However, I am then still faced with providing a rational explanation for her partial paralysis, of which there is concrete and tangible medical evidence. I first considered temporary sleep paralysis, of which there are records of extreme cases, but none of which had a duration anywhere as long as Lena's case. Then there is what is called periodic paralysis, one of the primary causes of which is stress. In essence, there is a breakdown in the chemical processes involved in muscle movement. Again, though, usually the dysfunction is short-lived, and does not require extended hospitalization. That left only hysteria or severe emotional trauma as a reasonable explanation. And neither seemed applicable. There was simply nothing on-going in her life at the time or one single event to provide for so extreme a reaction.

That left me to consider the less rational or plausible, of which the paranormal was front and center. Through my research, I discovered one of the supposed arts of the Skinwalker is rendering its victim unresponsive, which it accomplishes with the introduction of potent powders or dusts through the victim's mouth or nose. However, the Skinwalker is not known to accost random victims, but instead acts out of revenge. Lena did not recall offending anyone, nor did she have reason to believe Wayne had. That in itself was enough for me to discount the plausibility of the contemporary Skinwalker, but I also couldn't bring myself to seriously consider the whole human transforming concept—not in this day and age.

Nevertheless, at least for me, there is quite a gap between the Skinwalker implied by the lore of the indigenous peoples who first walked upon these lands and either the version which applies to the early 19th century or the one found in the local stories of today. While these more contemporary versions rely on man turning to beast and back again, the sooner believed the Skinwalker to be an entity from an alternate plane who moved in and out of our world through portals. For me, if there is any association between the Bishop family and a Skinwalker, it would be the one with the extraterrestrial or other dimension implication. My speculation, then, is that there was something at work in Lena's case beyond the self-imposed limitations of science, or at the very least, for which science would be willing to offer explanation. If pushed into the proverbial corner, I would accept a paranormal phenomenon as plausible cause, but I am not willing to go so far as to suggest a Skinwalker.

As far as Emma identifying one of these dimensional portals, I am limited by the fact that it was Lena who reported it and not Emma. Secondary sources by their nature lack the interpretive elements of the original source. For example, there is no way to accurately replicate facial expressions, tone and timbre of voice, body language, or any of the other nuances that contribute to interpretation. Not only that, but in terms of the investigative process, I can't fully discount the possibility that Emma didn't actually say what Lena said she said. Assuming, however, that the account is accurate, given the sophistication of what she said, it is not irrational to entertain the idea that some other source than her brother or his comic books put those words and the concept or images they convey into her head.

With regard to the poltergeist-like activity, I am going to refrain from any speculation. Regardless of any explanation I might offer, there are a thousand and one other possibilities equally as rational or irrational, depending on your perspective. Not only that, but the absence of any tangible forensic evidence, photos or audio recordings, for example, sort of makes it all irrelevant. I'll just say, instead, that the activity described was consistent with other reported encounters of this nature, and leave it at that.

This brings me then to Aaron. The supposed encounter with the small-sized Indian may very well have been a manifestation of the stimulus provided by the on-going activity and, no doubt, what his little ears were attending to while his parents thought otherwise and, as suggested by his father, having recently seen the movie *The Indian in the Cupboard*—which I only presume is the movie to which he was referring. It is also worth noting that like the action figure, similarly, the Indian reported by Aaron was absent genitalia. I am obligated to acknowledge, however, that the description of the Indian he claimed to have seen doesn't match the one in the movie, nor does the movie include any scenes even close to what he says he saw in terms of the wall, and what in my speculation I will refer to as an alternate dimension.

As for his encounter with the teen-aged girl, there is common reference in these parts to a similar spirit or ghost. As the tale goes, she was killed by violent means and now roams about looking for children to whom she initially presents as friendly, but then later lures them to their deaths. Her motive, it is believed, is to deprive her victims in the same way as she had been deprived, and in the process have them suffer the same pain she did.

While it is possible that Aaron, who presents as a bright and precocious boy, was aware, too, of this legend or myth, that wouldn't sufficiently explain the multiple incidents in which Tonto, the family dog, had aggressive reactions, and especially the window event. Lena, particularly under hypnosis, exhibited high degree of anxiety while recounting the event, and was both thoroughly convinced and convincing that Aaron was talking with someone who, for the purpose of my argument, presented as otherwise invisible or in spiritual form. That Tonto demonstrated such aggressive and directed behavior would seem to support the

In the Shadow of the Ridge

presence of an unseen entity, and make more of the incident than just Lena's imagination or Aaron's role playing.

Continuing, therefore, with my willingness to speculate, I can't ignore that Aaron due to his inquisitive nature and otherwise healthy and both gender and age appropriate preoccupation with UFOs, the horror genre, anything paranormal, video games, and graphic novels, was particularly susceptible to suggestion, and therefore elements of his encounters were in all likelihood a product of his imagination. That said, as these encounters did not occur in isolation—his mother as witness, the reactions of Tonto, and the other ongoing phenomenon in and around the house, I am willing to consider a paranormal presence, by which I mean the manifestation of a force or energy that is not normal.

And this brings me to the reservoir incident. The part of Lena's narrative which was most interesting was when describing her surroundings and what it was she was perceiving she makes no mention of any kind of alien or supernatural entity. Later in the debriefing session when she shares the conversation that she had post-incident with Maggie, Maggie, too, makes no mention of any entity. In fact, in both cases, it is not unreasonable to infer that both Lena and Maggie perceived themselves as alien to their own physical bodies, with both providing the perception of being at the same time aware of but distant from herself.

As Lena was first providing these details, I immediately equated it with my own experience with marijuana. For those not familiar, during the high there is often a resultant degree of sensory deprivation which can affect the way the brain interprets physical stimuli. One of the most common manifestations of this deprivation is a low-level hallucination in which the person perceives himself as distance from himself, often reported as sitting just outside of or beside one's own person. However, neither Lena nor Maggie were high at the time. So while the sensory perception might be similar, the mechanism responsible for that perception was not.

The other plausible explanation, of course, is the stress associated with Lena's sudden and unexpected loss of control of the vehicle and belief that they were going to smash into the rocks. Back when I was in college, I was involved in a fairly frightening collision. I was coming down an overpass. The light at the bottom was in the process of changing. As expected, I pressed down on the brake pedal. And nothing happened. To make a long story short, I attempted to avoid the movement of the cars in front of me—specifically those making a left onto the overpass from the side road at the bottom, and instead collided with one of them, which then sent me careening into a second. However, what I remember most about the incident, is while my car was bouncing around, it was as if I was totally disconnected from the incident; so much so, that if my life had been taken from me at that moment, I wouldn't have noticed. Was it possible that Lena and Maggie were simply experiencing something similar? Yes, it is. However, while I clearly recall details of the scene unfolding around me—the other cars, the intersection, the moment suspended in time, as it were, both Lena and Maggie, as reported by Lena, saw something entirely different than—and alien to—their actual physical environment.

My conclusion, therefore, is that, yes, it is plausible that they encountered a physical area of energy, which for a lack of a better word, could be referred to as a portal, a different plane, or an alternate dimension. Of course, I have no explanation for the presence of an existing field of energy fitting this definition.

Regardless, I find myself going back to something I first heard from Samantha, my fifteen year-old subject from when I first arrived in Vernal, and that was a reference to *her animal*. This is the same term that was used by Lena when reporting her encounter with two separate and distinct entities while in the hospital, and again later by Emma when she finally acknowledged the incident in the Cherokee. To me, only an entity alien to human beings and to corporeal beings, in general, would feel no need to distinguish between higher and lower order animals. Animals would be animals. That this entity would, however, prefer to house itself within the body of the highest order animal—a human being, for example—than in that of a lower order animal—a stray dog or a coyote, given its obvious degree of intelligence, and the physical needs it would then have, is also logical.

In other words, what I am offering as a plausible explanation to the events experienced by Lena and her family is the presence of an entity that is either extraterrestrial or paranormal, by which I mean inclusive of any presence other than extraterrestrial, and which interacts with us, meaning our kind, when it chooses by entering our physical space through portals of some sort, and as needed or desired, makes use of or attempts to make use, if only temporarily, the physical body, or animal, of those who present as most susceptible to that process.

Now while this is purely speculation on my part, I will offer the following as circumstantial evidence.

Following the conversation I had with Jessica the night I brought her Emma's gift, I, of course, arranged to speak to Lena. I asked her if she was aware of what it was that Emma intended to give to me. The expression on her face was one of confusion, and then she told me she was under the impression that Emma had something she wanted to tell me, and not something she wanted to give me. She remembered asking Emma only how it went, that Emma said 'good', and that, as she recalled, Emma was very quiet on the way home, but that she didn't think anything of it as Emma was usually quiet in the car. I then told her of the pendant, and asked if she would follow-up with it and get back to me.

She called me the very next day. She was clearly upset. I asked her if she would prefer to come to the office, that I'd be there, or she could come in when it was convenient. She said she was okay, and first prefacing that Emma became visibly frustrated during their conversation, she then related to me the following details. She said that Emma had no recollection of coming to my office, meeting with me, or speaking to me. When Lena tried to spark her memory, as it were, Emma became increasingly agitated and then visibly scared. She reported only that she remembered falling asleep in the car and then waking up just as they were pulling into the driveway. In addition, Emma thought it was silly that Lena would ask her my wife's name—she said she didn't know—or suggest that Emma would have given her a gift, and definitely not the pendant, which she was at the time wearing. Ultimately, I asked Lena a few questions, and even asked if she would be willing to bring Emma in for an evaluation. She said she would have to speak to Wayne, and she'd get back to me. To date, she hasn't done that, and I haven't pressed the matter.

I will, however, end with this. After I showed Jessica the pendant that night at the dinner table, and after we discussed all the possibilities as to how Emma may have gotten it, including the obvious, I then told her what Emma had said about the baby. I could tell she didn't quite know what to make of it, and was perhaps a little uneasy. Later that evening, as were watching television together and enjoying a beer, she said she thought she should mention that she had had one of her "woman" episodes that morning, after which I became concerned. We agreed she would make an appointment with the doctor.

Now, you can call it speculation or whatever you want, but on October 3, 2014, at 10:47 am, my wife Jessica gave birth to a healthy 7 pound, 7 ounce boy, who we named Garrett. As for the pendant Emma gave to my wife, or more accurately to the baby, we keep it in a small pouch in a jewelry box next to his bed—just in case.

ABOUT THE AUTHOR

Erick T. Rhetts grew up on the east coast of the United States of America. He attended multiple colleges and universities, eventually earning an undergraduate degree leading to a career he believed at the time to be relevant, and then additional Graduate degrees, furthering that perceived relevancy.

In his previous incarnations he worked at various endeavors, most of which paid well-enough, and from which he manages a comfortable, yet humble retirement, and at an age yet young enough to enjoy some of which life has to offer. That, of course, changes with each passing year and the all too rapidly encroaching inevitable.

As for his interest in the paranormal, and particularly Skinwalker Ranch, he recognizes no other origin than the Ranch itself. Not considering himself a formal investigator of the Ranch and its reported phenomena, but instead a collector of related stories and narratives, he is, nonetheless, fascinated by the very concept of a paranormal epicenter and making sense of the purpose or objective of any type of entity associated with just such a concept and location.

Currently, Mr. Rhetts splits his time both within and outside of the borders of the United States. He spends most of that time coming to terms with his predisposition for earthly pursuits—primarily a predisposition for spirits contained in bottles—which is not intended to imply Genies of any sort. When not so occupied, he writes the occasional book, his latest being the one you currently have in hand.

Printed in Great Britain
by Amazon